the 30-Minute VEGETARIAN COOKBOOK

the 30-Minute VEGETARIAN COOKBOOK

100 Healthy, Delicious Meals for Busy People

Lisa Turner

ROCKRIDGE
PRESS

Interior and Cover Designer: Amanda Kirk
Art Producer: Sue Smith
Editor: Daniel Grogan
Production Editor: Gleni Bartels
Production Manager: Holly Haydash
Photography: Andrew Purcell

ISBN: Print 978-1-64152-645-6 | eBook 978-1-64152-646-3

Jalapeño Frittata 28

CONTENTS

INTRODUCTION

These days, many of us lead such busy lives that mealtime often seems like one more chore to fit into our hectic schedules. Instead of cooking, we're tempted to grab takeout on the way home or buy preprepared dinners from the grocery store. But these premade meals are frequently loaded with processed ingredients and ample amounts of sugar and sodium, not to mention unhealthy oils, which leave us feeling sluggish. This way of eating takes a toll, not only on our budget, but more importantly on the long-term health and well-being of ourselves and our families. The good news is that, with a little planning, we can make a great many meals at home in just 30 minutes or less with delicious and nourishing results.

This is just as true for vegetarians as it is for meat eaters. I have been a vegetarian for more than 25 years, and I have embraced the challenge of juggling a busy lifestyle while incorporating quick and healthy cooking. Although I am passionate about cooking and enjoy spending time in the kitchen, there are times when I just want fast meal solutions. Armed with some basic tools and cooking fundamentals, I've found that I can make time for myself and my family, all while creating nourishing vegetarian meals that taste so good, you'd never guess that so little time was actually spent in the kitchen.

In *The 30-Minute Vegetarian Cookbook*, you'll find 100 easy recipes to make your everyday cooking a rewarding experience, as well as tips to make your kitchen time productive and efficient. First, to get started, try devoting a little time on your days off or weekends to drawing up meal plans for the week ahead in order to reduce the number of trips to the grocery store. You'll find advice here on what staples to have on hand in between shopping trips to make planning even easier. In addition to the many delicious recipes, you'll see that many sauces, dressings, and blends can be made ahead of time, so you can have them on hand when you just want to get a meal cooked and on the table in a hurry.

Whether you're already a vegetarian, considering a transition to a vegetarian diet, or just want to reduce the amount of meat that you eat, the recipes here are a handy and convenient reference for making food that goes far beyond just salads and pasta—they'll take you from breakfast to dinner to dessert, with snacks in between. In short, this book will give you many things: the tools to refresh your kitchen and dining life, a feeling of control over the quality of food that you serve, and a sense of accomplishment that you are feeding yourself and your family wholesome, nourishing, and delicious meals without taking away from spending time on yourself and them.

Mediterranean Pita Pizzas with Olives and Goat Cheese 131

Chapter 1 ⌒

FAST AND EASY VEGETARIAN MEALS

This chapter will provide you with a basic introduction to kitchen essentials and techniques to get you on the way to preparing nourishing and balanced vegetarian meals in your own kitchen. Planning ahead means minimizing the amount of time you spend cooking and maximizing your enjoyment of eating a home-cooked meal. This chapter will also be a handy reference tool as you become more comfortable in the kitchen and cook your way through this book. With the basics you'll find here and some experience in hand, you'll soon be making delicious and satisfying 30-minute meals as you begin to explore the creative and incredibly diverse world of vegetarian cooking.

Fast and Fresh in 30 Minutes

Whether you are a longtime vegetarian or are looking to begin the transition to a vegetarian diet, or simply looking to incorporate more vegetarian meals into your week, you'll find plenty of exciting recipes that are not only fast but fresh and delicious, too. You'll be pleasantly surprised when you discover how many different types of meals you can prepare. The recipes that follow range from breakfast ideas to quick lunch and dinner options, as well as some sweet treats and desserts. Many different types of ingredients are used and the recipes are inspired by different cuisines and styles of cooking, so you'll have plenty to choose from to keep your meals interesting and varied.

To give you an idea of just a few of the recipes in this book: You'll find beautiful, classic simplicity, from a hearty Tex-Mex Chili (page 123) or a fragrant Indian-inspired Simple Lemon Dal (page 97) to a sumptuous Creamy Polenta with Sautéed Mixed Mushrooms (page 99). There are also plenty of dishes that will be sure to wow your family or guests without letting on that you spent so little time in the kitchen, such as a truly amazing Hummus Pizza (page 137), a lovely Spanish-Style Saffron Rice with Black Beans (page 96), or an elegant Pasta with Roasted Brussels Sprouts and Creamy Cashew Alfredo Sauce (page 84). And if you like to finish off your meal with something sweet, you'll also find an incredibly easy Pumpkin Pie Pudding (page 169), a refreshing Peach-Lime Lassi (page 166), and a rich Chocolate Mug Cake (page 171). All in just 30 minutes or less!

PROTEIN COMPARISONS

One of the questions most frequently asked of vegetarians is "Just where do you get your protein?" Well, protein is actually incredibly easy for vegetarians to obtain. Beans and legumes are protein-packed and, when paired with a grain, provide a balanced protein-based meal. Nuts and seeds are also protein-rich, as are leafy greens and a wide selection of other vegetables. Scattering a tablespoon of hemp seeds over your breakfast cereal and salads, or whisking them into dressings, will add nine grams of protein without any effort or alteration of taste. Quinoa, like hemp seeds, is a complete source of protein because it contains all nine essential amino acids. Dairy products are also rich sources of proteins and other nutrients. A well-balanced vegetarian diet that includes a range of foods from these sources throughout the day will ensure you are getting plenty of protein, as well as fiber and other essential vitamins and minerals.

Let's have a look at some of the common proteins available in an omnivorous diet compared to some alternatives in a vegetarian diet.

Meat	Protein	Vegetarian Comparisons	Protein
3 ounces steak	25 grams	1 cup cooked chickpeas	18 grams
3 ounces chicken breast	26 grams	1 cup cooked lentils	24 grams
3.5 ounces frozen beef patty	15 grams	2 large eggs	12 grams
3 ounces chicken thigh	20 grams	3 ounces Cheddar cheese	21 grams
4 ounces salmon	27 grams	1 cup Greek yogurt	23 grams
3 ounces ham	19 grams	1 cup cooked quinoa	8 grams
2 bacon strips	3 grams	2 tablespoons peanut butter	8 grams
2 breakfast sausages	5 grams	3 ounces tempeh	16 grams

Plant-Based Goodness

As people become more health-conscious and concerned about the long- and short-term effects of what they eat, a leaner and cleaner diet—one that isn't laden with preservatives and other artificial ingredients and is more focused on plant-based sources and meals—has led to an increase in the popularity of a vegetarian diet. Ethical considerations, including concerns for animal welfare under modern agricultural practices, are what often make people begin to think of moving toward a plant-based diet. The use of hormones and antibiotic treatments in farmed animals also leads many people to consider whether they really know what they're putting in their bodies when they eat meat. After all, we like to know what we're actually eating, don't we?

These ideas certainly influenced me in my own decision to become a vegetarian. I can attest from personal experience that one of the first things I noticed, shortly after switching to a vegetarian diet, was how much "cleaner" I felt. Meals became easier to digest. It wasn't because I wasn't eating enough—my body just didn't have to work as hard to break down the nutrients in a plant-focused diet. If the benefits of avoiding meat for health and ethical reasons weren't enough, it turns out that vegetarian eating can often be far more economical. Legumes and grains form the bulk of protein sources for vegetarians and are low-cost and versatile alternatives to meat.

When I became a vegetarian more than 25 years ago, it was much more challenging to find quality, informative vegetarian cookbooks, especially ones that provided guidance for balanced and healthy meals. Things have changed greatly since then, and there has been a marked increase in the number of different foods available at local supermarkets that make vegetarian meals even easier to prepare.

The Challenge of Time

Many people are concerned about the question of preparation time and the idea that making satisfying vegetarian meals is much more work than those where meat or fish is the primary focus and protein source. Happily, this is not the case. Once you get organized, get your kitchen stocked with the essentials, and master a few basic skills, making delicious and fast meals is easier than you might think.

For example, if you are using canned beans for one of your recipes, a dish where they are featured can actually take less time than a meat-based recipe, as the beans are already cooked and ready to use. Further, cooking with beans often requires much less critical attention to timing and temperature than cooking with meat. Supermarkets also offer many other preprepared options, such as prewashed and chopped fresh vegetables. Explore further and you'll find a great variety of healthy prepared dips, sauces, and condiments to make cooking faster and easier.

There are other ways that time in the kitchen can be spent productively and efficiently without having to be an expert cook. Not only do precut vegetables reduce the amount of time you spend prepping, but with some practice, you will find that certain tasks become much faster. The more times you chop an onion, the better you'll get at it! While waiting for something to simmer, you can prepare a dressing or sauce, wipe up surfaces, or clean dishes. Taking a few moments in the beginning to review your recipe and gather all of the ingredients that you need will help you organize your thoughts and workspace. This will reduce distractions and the amount of time you spend running back and forth between the cupboards or refrigerator and the stove.

COOKING FASTER: TIPS FROM THE PROS

» **Start with a clean and tidy kitchen.** Unwashed dishes and a cluttered workspace will only detract from your focus and slow you down. This will also make cleanup easier and faster after dinner. Best of all, a clean, uncluttered kitchen will put you in the right frame of mind for making something creative, nourishing, and enjoyable.

» **Before cooking, read though the recipe.** Make sure you have everything you need and that you understand the cooking steps. You don't want to start making a recipe, only to realize that you are out of a key ingredient or don't have an essential piece of equipment.

» **Assemble all of the recipe ingredients.** Having everything at hand before you start cooking will keep you from wasting time searching for those cans of tomatoes or spice jars that might be buried at the back of a cupboard when you want your focus to be on cooking.

» **Get all the equipment out.** Gather and put in place all the pieces you'll need before using them, such as lining baking sheets with parchment paper. Digging for pans in the middle of cooking can throw off your timing, especially if you find that they need wiping down before use.

» **Learn to roughly measure spices.** While some recipes do require more precise measurements, many ingredients, such as spices and basic seasonings, may be roughly eyeballed. As you gain more experience cooking, this becomes easier. In the meantime, this prep step saves you the time of measuring each and every ingredient.

» **Prep and clean as you go.** In many cases, you'll find yourself waiting for something to cook or bake, and that's time you can spend preparing other parts of the recipe. If there is nothing further to prep, clean up some of the dishes you may have dirtied in the meantime.

The Convenient Vegetarian Kitchen

Modern cooks have the luxury of having many kinds of time-saving kitchen equipment available to them. Not only will you love the convenience of easy cleanup that the newest nonstick pans give you, but they're also tolerant of high heat and save time and effort as they help keep food from sticking. Today's food processors and high-powered blenders make mixing ingredients a breeze. It's worthwhile to invest in some of these pieces of equipment, even if you are only an occasional cook, because well-made implements and machines should last years in the kitchen. The accumulated savings in time will far outweigh the up-front cost and the frustrations of using manual methods or inefficient equipment.

Essential Equipment

♦ **Knives (3).** In addition to a paring knife, a good sharp chef's knife is an especially useful tool to have, as it makes prep faster and easier. A dull knife is cumbersome and frustrating, especially when you are dealing with harder fruits and vegetables like potatoes or squashes, or even staple ingredients such as onions and tomatoes. You'll also want a trusty bread knife.

♦ **Skillet (2).** Try to get a large one and a medium one, both preferably nonstick, because they make cleanup and cooking easier. There are many safe and more durable alternatives to Teflon on the market these days, such as ceramic.

♦ **Pots.** You'll want a selection of saucepans of varying sizes, preferably nonstick. As with nonstick skillets, cleanup is easier and decreases the likelihood you'll have to scrape crusted or burned food from the pan, so the whole cooking process will go more smoothly. You'll also want a good-size soup pot.

♦ **Sheet pan (1).** A standard nonstick baking sheet is something you'll use often for both cooking and baking. More than one is preferable, but not essential.

♦ **Baking dish (4).** Ideally, you'll want a good-size Pyrex or ceramic casserole dish, a 9-by-13-inch glass baking dish, an 8-by-8-inch baking pan, and a glass or nonstick metal pie dish.

♦ **Muffin pan.** Look for a standard 12-cup tin for both savory and sweet creations.

♦ **Blender and/or immersion blender.** If you can afford it, it's worthwhile to invest in a high-powered blender. It's an invaluable tool for making sauces, dips, and dressings. In addition, an immersion blender is useful for blending soups and sauces right in the cook pot, saving time because you don't have to pour the contents of your pot into a blender or food processor bowl.

♦ **Measuring tools and mixing bowls.** A set of measuring cups, ranging from ¼ cup to 1 cup, is indispensable. Similarly, you'll want a set of measuring spoons, ranging from ⅛ teaspoon to 1 tablespoon. Also handy are a set of glass or metal bowls of varying sizes.

♦ **Metal strainer.** Look for a sturdy fine-mesh strainer for rinsing beans and lentils and for draining cooked foods such as pasta and noodles.

♦ **Spoons, spatulas, and a whisk.** In addition to a few wooden spoons, you'll want a set of implements, such as spatulas and a whisk, that work with your cookware. Note that some nonstick pots and pans are not suited for metal implements, but there are some good, inexpensive, and durable heatproof, BPA-free, nylon accessories that will work for all your cooking needs.

♦ **Cutting boards (2).** A small one comes in especially handy for chopping smaller items, while a large one is essential for all of your chopping needs. The boards I use are wooden and fairly lightweight.

♦ **Aluminum foil and parchment paper.** Aluminum foil is handy for lining pans and for wrapping food for baking or reheating. Parchment paper not only makes cleanup easier but also prevents food from sticking to roasting pans and burning.

Gadgets for People Who Hate Prep

In addition to essential equipment, there are plenty of inexpensive gadgets and tools that are especially useful to have. The following is a list of items that are not essential to have on hand, but they certainly cut down on the time spent prepping a meal so you can get down to the serious business of cooking.

♦ **Hand-mixer.** In some cases, a hand-mixer can be used in place of a whisk. It cuts down on the arm work and speeds up the process.

♦ **Food processor.** I personally find this to be essential in my kitchen, as it is very handy for making dips and sauces, and also for quickly chopping vegetables.

♦ **Cheese grater.** In addition to grating cheese, you can use it to grate many items, such as garlic and ginger, rather than mincing them.

♦ **Potato masher.** Apart from its obvious use, it's a great tool for mashing other cooked vegetables and even beans, if required for a recipe.

♦ **Vegetable peeler.** Though not essential, a sharp peeler is ideal for vegetables such as potatoes or carrots. It is much faster than using a knife in most cases.

♦ **Garlic press.** A strong garlic press makes the job of mincing garlic a breeze.

♦ **Pastry brush.** A silicone pastry brush can be had for as little as a dollar and is very easy to clean. A great tool for greasing cookware and pans quickly, pastry brushes are also useful for brushing oil or egg whites over pastries and breads.

♦ **Tiny bowls.** These are one of my favorite time-saving tools. I use them for having premeasured spices and chopped ingredients ready on hand while cooking.

Time-Saving Ingredients

Becoming an efficient home cook who can make and plate delicious wholesome meals in little time starts with having a kitchen stocked with staple ingredients that will make your shopping, planning, and cooking easier. Many common ingredients that can be made from fresh can also be found in jars or cans that will make prep time take no time at all. Here are some great ways to keep these ingredients on hand without having to worry about fresh ingredients spoiling.

Pantry

♦ **Oils and vinegars.** Olive oil, sesame oil, and coconut oil, as well as white vinegar and red wine vinegar, are essential ingredients for many recipes.

♦ **Canned and jarred goods.** A selection of canned beans—including chickpeas, pinto beans, black beans, and black-eyed peas—and lentils can be useful to have on hand. Canned tomatoes form the basis of many vegetarian recipes. Canned or jarred tomato sauces, salsas, or other sauces also help make it easy to put together a quick dinner in a pinch. Nut butters, such as peanut or almond, come in jars and add creaminess, flavor, and protein.

♦ **Dried beans and grains.** Grains such as rice, quinoa, and couscous help quickly fill out a meal and balance proteins and nutrients. Dried beans or lentils are useful to have on hand, and they're even cheaper than canned.

♦ **Nuts and seeds.** These items often figure into recipes, are great for a high-protein snacks, and may be sprinkled on dishes to add extra protein and flavor.

♦ **Dried pastas and noodles.** These are great for putting together a really fast meal without having planned ahead.

- **All-purpose flour.** This is great to keep around because it doesn't need to be refrigerated and will keep for a long time in your pantry.

- **Hardier fruits and vegetables.** There are many long-lasting vegetables that do not require refrigeration, such as potatoes, yams, and onions.

- **Spices and dried herbs.** A selection of your favorite seasonings—such as turmeric, chili powder, cumin, coriander, cinnamon, dried herbs, and crushed red pepper flakes—will make your dishes more flavorful and vibrant.

Fridge

- **A selection of fresh fruits and vegetables.** Tomatoes, lemons, carrots, garlic, and fresh ginger will usually keep in your crisper for over a week and give you plenty of options when considering easy meal plans. Apples, pears, and oranges are refreshing snacks when you need a quick burst of energy and hydration.

- **Eggs, plain whole yogurt, and cheese.** These are terrific sources of protein and other nutrients and are easy to use with other ingredients in recipes or just on their own.

- **Milk or non-dairy milk.** Even if you don't drink milk on its own, milk or non-dairy milks are used in soups and sauces to add creaminess. Non-dairy milks—such as almond, soy, and coconut milk—keep much longer than dairy milk and are often sold sweetened or flavored, but unsweetened and unflavored milks are easy to find, too.

- **Sauces and condiments.** Many of these require refrigeration after opening, such as ketchup, tomato sauces, salsas, tamari or soy sauce, jarred olives, and sun-dried tomatoes.

- **Whole-wheat flour.** Unlike all-purpose flour, whole-wheat flour should be refrigerated to prevent it from becoming rancid over time.

♦ **Frozen vegetables.** Many vegetables found in the supermarket freezer section, such as green peas and corn, make for easy and colorful additions to soups, stews, and cooked rice.

♦ **Breads, pita breads, flatbreads, and other baked goods.** You can store these in the freezer in order to keep them from getting stale. Leftover baked goods such as muffins and cookies will also keep in the freezer.

♦ **Prepared or leftover sauces.** Many homemade sauces, such as tomato sauce, will keep in freezer bags ready for quick thawing in a microwave or in a bowl of hot water.

♦ **Soups and broths.** Leftovers from dinners can be stored in plastic containers in a freezer for reheating at a later date.

♦ **Cooked pastas.** These can also be frozen for quick reheating. Make sure to let the pasta cool before freezing and store separately from any pasta sauce you may have made. Drizzle a little olive oil over the cooled pasta to keep the noodles from sticking together, and then freeze in airtight containers or freezer bags for up to two weeks.

After prepping food, I think most of us would agree that cleanup is probably not the most enjoyable kitchen chore, but I've gathered a collection of simple tips that make it a far less dreadful task. Here are five ways to make it even easier.

» Use parchment paper for lining sheet pans. In addition to saving you the trouble of scrubbing food residue from the pan after cooking, it ensures food browns more evenly and is less likely to burn.

» Rinse dishes as you finish with them and stack them neatly beside the sink or put them in your dishwasher.

» Sometimes, when you are waiting for something to cook or bake that requires little attention, you can start washing some of the dishes you no longer need.

» While you are enjoying your dinner, cookware can be soaked in dishwater or hot water to make scouring the pots faster.

» Use cookware-appropriate scouring pads or sponges. If you use nonstick cookware, these aren't usually necessary.

About the Recipes

My sincere hope is that these recipes will inspire you to explore the wonders, variety, and wealth of health benefits that a vegetarian diet offers. Consider the recipes as templates to alter, adorn, or even simplify further in order to suit your needs and preferences. Add more seasonings or other ingredients, for instance, or change up the grains, beans, and vegetables used in each dish. The possibilities are endless.

As you already know, the recipes in this book are all designed to be made in 30 minutes or less, including the prep time involved. Each chapter is organized to begin with recipes that are the least complicated and proceed to dishes that require a bit more advanced knowledge and confidence (but not too much!). To make things even handier for you, each recipe includes time-saving information that is specific to each meal.

Dietary labels. Each of the recipes comes with the following dietary labels, so you can quickly choose recipes according to dietary restrictions or preferences. You'll see the following labels: Vegan, Gluten-Free, Dairy-Free, Nut-Free, Oil-Free, and Soy-Free. Recipes labeled as vegan often include a note or tip on how to ensure that the recipe is truly that. Also, many of the recipes that aren't labeled as gluten-free can be adapted to be made so by swapping in gluten-free pastas, breads, and wraps.

Tips that make it even easier. In some recipes, you'll find explanations of some of the ingredients used that you may not be familiar with, together with substitution options. In other cases, where an ingredient is used that will require more prep than perhaps you have time for, suggestions are offered to reduce the number of steps and time spent on making the meal. When relevant, cooking hacks and techniques are provided as well to simplify and speed things up further—for example, kitchen gadgets and tricks that make time-consuming tasks simple and quick. Information on how best to store and reheat leftovers is also included to make your meals last longer.

Sometimes flavor and protein enhancements are suggested. Adding different spices or vegetables as well as changing up beans and legumes, or garnishing your dishes with some chopped nuts, seeds, or other seasonings—these options are offered up for your consideration. Even a prepared sauce or dish can be dressed up with minimal effort. Lastly, serving suggestions will help you present meals with ease. Enjoy!

Mixed-Berry Cornmeal Muffins 32

Chapter 2

BREAKFAST

Breakfast is one of the most important meals of the day. A protein-packed breakfast provides the fuel your body needs to kick-start the day. In this chapter, you'll find recipes for when you have little time to spare in the morning but want something more substantial and nourishing than a simple bowl of cereal. Some of the recipes require a bit more attention and patience, but still take less than 30 minutes to prepare. There is no reason to think this chapter is only designed for your breakfast needs, either. As all of the recipes have a significant amount of protein, which is essential to all of your meals, they are also well-suited for a light lunch or dinner. Aren't eggs and pancakes just as enjoyable and satisfying later in the day, too?

Peanut Butter Oatmeal

VEGAN, GLUTEN-FREE, DAIRY-FREE, SOY-FREE
SERVES 2 • PREP TIME: 5 MINUTES • COOK TIME: 10 MINUTES

Oatmeal is one of the most comforting and easy ways to start the day. This dressed-up version takes only a few minutes longer to prepare than basic oatmeal. Protein-rich peanut butter and coconut milk are stirred into the cooking water for an extra-creamy and flavorful bowl of oats. Use either crunchy or smooth peanut butter for this recipe—though I prefer crunchy peanut butter, because it adds a pleasant complementary contrast in textures.

⅔ cup coconut milk or almond milk

1½ cups water

⅓ cup natural peanut butter

¼ teaspoon ground cinnamon

1 cup rolled oats

½ teaspoon vanilla extract

1 or 2 tablespoons honey or maple syrup (optional)

1. Combine the coconut milk, water, peanut butter, and cinnamon in a small saucepan.

2. Bring to a boil over medium heat, stirring continually to incorporate the peanut butter.

3. As soon as the mixture comes to a boil, stir in the oats and vanilla extract, and immediately reduce the heat to low.

4. Cook, stirring constantly, for 5 minutes, or until the oatmeal has thickened to taste. Add a bit more water or coconut milk if the mixture seems too thick.

5. Stir in the honey or maple syrup, if using, and serve immediately. Note that if using honey, this recipe will no longer be vegan.

SERVING TIP: To add additional flavor and protein, sprinkle with some hemp seeds or toasted almonds, or stir in some raisins or diced apple.

PER SERVING: Calories: 452; Total fat: 26g; Total carbs: 37g; Fiber: 8g; Sugar: 3g; Protein: 20g; Sodium: 124mg

Quinoa Porridge
with Honeyed Almonds

GLUTEN-FREE, OIL-FREE, SOY-FREE
SERVES 2 ● PREP TIME: 5 MINUTES ● COOK TIME: 15 MINUTES

Quinoa is one of the few plant foods that is a complete protein in itself, but vegetarians don't need the nutritional motivation to enjoy quinoa. Its light, nutty taste, versatility, and easy cooking make it a simple, delicious, and healthy alternative in a variety of grain recipes, including this breakfast porridge. Quick-roasted honeyed almonds, dried cranberries, and just a couple of spices make this an amazing alternative to the usual breakfast oatmeal.

For the almonds

½ cup raw almonds, chopped

2 tablespoons honey

For the quinoa

1 cup dried quinoa

1¼ cups milk or almond milk

1 cup water

1 (2-inch) cinnamon stick

¼ teaspoon ground cardamom (optional)

¼ cup dried cranberries

2 tablespoons honey

To make the almonds

1. Preheat the oven to 350°F.

2. Line a sheet pan with parchment paper.

3. Stir the almonds and honey together in a mixing bowl until the almonds are coated.

4. Spread the almonds over the lined sheet pan and roast for 5 to 10 minutes. Remove from the oven and allow to cool.

To make the quinoa

1. While the almonds are in the oven, add the quinoa to a medium saucepan and pour in the milk and water. Add the cinnamon stick and stir in the ground cardamom, if using, and dried cranberries.

continued ➤

2. Bring to a boil, then immediately reduce the heat to low and cover the saucepan.

3. Cook for 15 minutes.

4. Remove from the heat, discard the cinnamon stick, and stir in the honey.

5. Ladle into two bowls and top with the honeyed roasted almonds.

SUBSTITUTION TIP: Preprepared sliced, blanched almonds may be used in place of raw almonds without the need for chopping. You can also use ¼ teaspoon ground cinnamon in place of the cinnamon stick.

PER SERVING: Calories: 720; Total fat: 23g; Total carbs: 113g; Fiber: 10g; Sugar: 50g; Protein: 23g; Sodium: 66mg

Baked Avocado and Egg
with Miso Butter

GLUTEN-FREE, NUT-FREE, OIL-FREE
SERVES 2 • PREP TIME: 5 MINUTES • COOK TIME: 20 MINUTES

These baked avocado halves with eggs are quick and easy to prepare and perfect for breakfast or a light meal. There's no need to take the skin off the avocado either, as it serves as the bowl for eating. Satisfying and deliciously seasoned, the sweet and salty miso butter adds extra flavor and flair and can be whipped up while you wait for the eggs to bake. Loaded with protein and other nutritional benefits, this recipe can easily be doubled.

For the avocado and egg

1 avocado, halved and pitted

2 small eggs

1 fresh green chile, seeded and cut into thin strips

Chili powder or paprika

For the miso butter

1 tablespoon white (*shiro*) or other miso

½ teaspoon rice or white wine vinegar

¼ teaspoon cayenne pepper (optional)

To make the avocado and egg

1. Preheat the oven to 425°F. Line a baking sheet with parchment paper.

2. Scoop some of the flesh from the center of the avocado into a small bowl to reserve for the miso butter. The hollow of the avocado should be large enough to hold the egg.

3. Put two pieces of foil on the baking sheet and shape into nests to hold the avocados. Place the avocado halves into the nests.

4. Break an egg into each avocado half.

5. Bake for 10 to 20 minutes, until the egg is set.

continued ➤

To make the miso butter

1. While the avocado and eggs are baking, mash the reserved avocado flesh with a fork and stir in the miso, rice vinegar, and cayenne, if using. The mixture should have the consistency of a fairly thin butter. Add a bit of water if the mixture seems too thick.

2. Remove the avocado halves from the oven and transfer to serving plates.

3. Spoon the miso butter over the tops in a crisscross pattern and garnish with green chile strips and a sprinkle of chili powder or paprika.

4. Serve immediately.

TECHNIQUE TIP: To cut and pit an avocado, make a lengthwise cut from top to bottom around the pit with a sharp, sturdy knife. Twist the avocado to separate the halves. You should be able to nudge the pit right out of the halves with your fingers or with the aid of a spoon.

PER SERVING: Calories: 217; Total fat: 18g; Total carbs: 10g; Fiber: 7g; Sugar: 1g; Protein: 7g; Sodium: 379mg

Mushroom and Jalapeño Breakfast Hash

VEGAN, GLUTEN-FREE, DAIRY-FREE, NUT-FREE, SOY-FREE
SERVES 2 • PREP TIME: 10 MINUTES • COOK TIME: 20 MINUTES

Earthy mushrooms and hot jalapeño peppers combine with a traditional potato and onion hash in this easy yet incredibly flavorful breakfast that comes together in just one pan with little preparation time.

4 tablespoons extra-virgin olive oil

1 medium onion, cut into ¼-inch-thick slices

1 large potato, cut into ½-inch cubes

2 jalapeño peppers, seeded and chopped

1 (8-ounce) package mushrooms, chopped

Salt

Freshly ground black pepper

1. Heat the olive oil in a large skillet over medium-high heat. When hot, add the onions and sauté for 5 minutes, until the onions are softened and begin to brown on the edges.

2. Reduce the heat to medium and add the potatoes to the pan.

3. Cook for another 10 to 12 minutes, stirring occasionally, until the potatoes are tender and begin to brown evenly on all sides.

4. Stir in the jalapeño peppers and mushrooms and cook for another 5 minutes, stirring often.

5. Season with salt and pepper and serve immediately.

SERVING TIP: Double the recipe to increase the number of servings, though you will want to add 10 minutes to the cook time to ensure the potatoes cook throughout.

PER SERVING: Calories: 433; Total fat: 29g; Total carbs: 42g; Fiber: 7g; Sugar: 7g; Protein: 8g; Sodium: 97mg

Greek Omelet

GLUTEN-FREE, NUT-FREE, SOY-FREE
SERVES 2 • PREP TIME: 5 MINUTES • COOK TIME: 15 MINUTES

Omelets are a staple morning menu item at restaurants, not only because they're an attractive way to combine vegetables, cheese, and eggs into a filling and delicious breakfast, but also because they're a dish that many people are afraid to try at home. Omelets are actually very easy to make. All you need is a good nonstick skillet and a few simple tricks provided in this recipe for a colorful spinach, feta cheese, tomato, and olive version.

2 cups fresh spinach leaves, chopped

2 green onions, white and green parts, sliced

4 large eggs

½ teaspoon dried oregano

2 tablespoons extra-virgin olive oil

½ cup feta cheese, crumbled and divided

½ cup grape tomatoes, halved

½ cup sliced black or Kalamata olives

1. Heat a large nonstick skillet over medium-low heat and toss in the spinach leaves and the white parts of the green onion. Add a few teaspoons of water and cook, stirring frequently, for 8 to 10 minutes, or until the spinach leaves are wilted.

2. Transfer the spinach mixture to a bowl and set aside.

3. Remove the skillet from the heat and wipe with a paper towel.

4. While the spinach is cooking, break the eggs into a bowl and add the green parts of the green onions and the oregano. Beat lightly with a fork.

5. Return the skillet to the stove, add the olive oil, and turn up the heat to medium.

6. When the oil is hot, pour in the eggs and stir gently with the back of a fork for 30 seconds. Cook for 2 to 3 minutes or until the eggs are almost set, loosening the edges occasionally with a spatula and gently tilting the skillet to let the uncooked eggs reach the surface of the skillet.

7. Add the spinach mixture, ¼ cup of the feta cheese, grape tomatoes, and olives to the middle of the omelet. Let the eggs cook for another 20 to 30 seconds, until they're set.

8. Tap the handle of the pan sharply with your fist to loosen the omelet and then fold it over the spinach, cheese, tomatoes, and olives with a fork or spatula.

9. Slide the omelet onto a plate and scatter the remaining ¼ cup of feta cheese over top. Cut the omelet into two halves and serve immediately.

SUBSTITUTION TIP: One (16-ounce) package of frozen chopped spinach can be used instead of fresh. Defrost first by running the frozen spinach under warm water in a strainer or microwaving for 1 to 2 minutes until the spinach is soft. Wrap a paper towel around the spinach and squeeze the excess water out over a sink.

PER SERVING: Calories: 422; Total fat: 36g; Total carbs: 9g; Fiber: 3g; Sugar: 4g; Protein: 20g; Sodium: 880mg

Spicy Baked Egg Muffins

GLUTEN-FREE, NUT-FREE, SOY-FREE
MAKES 8 MUFFINS • PREP TIME: 5 MINUTES • COOK TIME: 20 MINUTES,
PLUS 5 MINUTES TO COOL

Technically not muffins, these egg and ricotta rounds made in a muffin tin are like spicy mini quiches. An ideal protein-packed breakfast, these muffins are also a wonderful portable snack. While they're delightful served as-is right from the oven, you could consider serving them with some salsa or a dollop of yogurt or sour cream for even more protein, or drizzling on your favorite hot sauce for additional heat.

Oil or nonstick cooking spray, for greasing the pan

8 large eggs

1 cup whole milk ricotta cheese

½ teaspoon cayenne pepper

½ teaspoon salt

2 green onions, white and green parts, thinly sliced

¼ cup cherry tomatoes, chopped

1 jalapeño pepper, seeded and minced (optional)

Freshly ground black pepper

¼ to ⅓ cup Monterey Jack cheese, grated

1. Preheat the oven to 350°F. Grease 8 cups of a standard 12-cup muffin tray with oil.

2. In a large bowl, whisk the eggs, ricotta cheese, cayenne pepper, and salt until smooth.

3. Stir in the green onions, tomatoes, jalapeño pepper, if using, and plenty of black pepper.

4. Pour the egg mixture into the prepared muffin cups.

5. Bake for 10 minutes.

6. Remove the pan from the oven and sprinkle the grated cheese evenly over the muffins.

7. Return the pan to the oven and bake for another 12 minutes, until the tops are puffy and browned and the muffins are firm to the touch.

8. Remove the tray from the oven and let cool for 5 minutes.

9. Run a sharp knife around the edges of each muffin to loosen them and gently nudge each muffin onto a serving plate.

10. Serve warm or at room temperature.

TECHNIQUE TIP: Instead of combining the eggs and ricotta with a whisk, use an electric hand-mixer or a blender and blend until smooth.

SUBSTITUTION TIP: If you don't have Monterey Jack on hand, then use Cheddar or mozzarella cheese instead.

PER SERVING: Calories: 130; Total fat: 9g; Total carbs: 3g; Fiber: 0g; Sugar: 1g; Protein: 11g; Sodium: 267mg

Jalapeño Frittata

GLUTEN-FREE, NUT-FREE, SOY-FREE
SERVES 4 TO 6 • PREP TIME: 5 MINUTES • COOK TIME: 25 MINUTES

Frittatas are an elegant way to serve up eggs, and they're far easier to make than most people imagine if you have a cast iron or oven-safe skillet. Cooked in the oven, there's no need to worry about flipping your frittata onto a plate. Don't let the idea of using 12 jalapeños scare you off. When they're baked with the eggs and cheese, the heat is mellow and pleasant.

8 large eggs

12 fresh jalapeño peppers, seeded and sliced into rounds

1½ cups grated aged Cheddar cheese, divided

2 tablespoons extra-virgin olive oil

1 onion, sliced

1 cup grape tomatoes

1 tablespoon fresh basil leaves, chopped or torn

1. Preheat the oven to 375°F.

2. Break the eggs into a large mixing bowl and beat well with a whisk. Add the jalapeño peppers and 1 cup of the Cheddar cheese, and mix until combined.

3. Meanwhile, heat the olive oil in a 10-inch cast iron or oven-safe skillet over medium heat. When hot, add the onion and fry for 3 to 4 minutes, until soft.

4. Add the grape tomatoes and stir for 1 minute. Toss in the basil and stir for a few seconds.

5. Stir in the egg mixture and let cook undisturbed for 4 minutes to let the bottom set.

6. Transfer the skillet to the oven and bake for 15 minutes, or until the eggs are set in the center, which you can test with a cake tester or a toothpick.

7. As soon as the frittata is set, turn on the broiler and move the oven rack up to the top level. Remove the frittata from the oven, sprinkle the last ½ cup of Cheddar cheese over the top, and place the skillet under the broiler for a couple of minutes, until the cheese is bubbling and the top is nicely browned.

8. Remove the pan from the oven. Run a rubber spatula around the edges of the pan to loosen the sides, then slide onto a large serving plate. Cut into wedges and serve hot.

SUBSTITUTION TIP: Sliced pickled jalapeños in jars and bagged pre-grated Cheddar cheese can be purchased in supermarkets to save time slicing and grating. Use 1 teaspoon dried basil in place of the fresh basil.

PER SERVING: Calories: 406; Total fat: 31g; Total carbs: 8g; Fiber: 2g; Sugar: 5g; Protein: 25g; Sodium: 408mg

Lemon Curd–Ricotta Pancakes

NUT-FREE, SOY-FREE
MAKES 4 (6-INCH) PANCAKES • PREP TIME: 10 MINUTES • COOK TIME: 15 MINUTES

These sturdy and hearty, protein-rich pancakes are delicately flavored with zesty lemon curd, so no additional sweetener is necessary. Blissfully fragrant and comforting, they are especially warming on a chilly morning. Serve hot from the pan and topped with warmed lemon curd or maple syrup, whipped cream, and some fresh berries for extra flavor and nutrients. Sweetened with enough toppings, you could even serve these for dessert.

4 large eggs, separated

1¼ cups ricotta cheese

2½ tablespoons prepared lemon curd

1⅓ cups all-purpose flour

Oil or nonstick cooking spray, for greasing the pan

1. In a small mixing bowl, beat the egg whites until stiff peaks form.

2. In a large mixing bowl, whisk together the egg yolks, ricotta cheese, and lemon curd. Add the flour and stir to combine.

3. Add the egg whites and, using a spatula, fold the mixture up and over itself until the ingredients are just combined, slowly rotating the bowl as you do so.

4. Heat a lightly greased large skillet over medium heat. When hot, scoop ¼ to ⅓ cup of the batter into the skillet for each pancake and use the back of a spoon or the scoop to spread the batter into a circular shape.

5. Cook for 3 to 4 minutes, until the bottoms of the pancakes turn golden brown. Flip the pancakes and cook for another 3 to 4 minutes until golden on both sides and the pancakes are cooked throughout. Repeat with the remaining batter, adding a bit more oil to the skillet as needed to prevent the pancakes from sticking.

6. Serve immediately.

TECHNIQUE TIP: To separate the eggs, hold a slotted spoon over a small bowl. Carefully break the egg over the slotted spoon and gently twist the spoon until the egg white runs through to the bowl. Transfer the yolk to another bowl.

PER SERVING: Calories: 314; Total fat: 13g; Total carbs: 32g; Fiber: 1g; Sugar: 3g; Protein: 18g; Sodium: 173mg

Baked Whole-Wheat Strawberry and Blueberry Pancakes

NUT-FREE, SOY-FREE

SERVES 6 • PREP TIME: 5 MINUTES • COOK TIME: 20 MINUTES

This is a highly attractive dish that is deceptively easy to prepare. These pancakes are soft and creamy, with a light, crispy exterior. They are also baked rather than fried, saving on actual hands-on time in the kitchen.

2 tablespoons unsalted butter

4 eggs, separated

1 cup whole-wheat flour

1 cup plain whole yogurt

2 tablespoons sugar

1 teaspoon vanilla extract

½ teaspoon baking powder

2 cups strawberries, halved or quartered

2 cups blueberries

Powdered sugar, for dusting (optional)

1. Preheat the oven to 450°F.

2. Put a tablespoon of butter each into two 9-inch pie dishes and place in the oven to melt the butter.

3. In a small bowl, beat the egg whites until stiff peaks form.

4. In a medium mixing bowl, whisk together the egg yolks, flour, yogurt, sugar, vanilla extract, and baking powder until well combined.

5. Add the egg whites and, using a spatula, fold the mixture up and over itself until the ingredients are just combined, slowly rotating the bowl as you do so.

6. Remove the pie dishes from the oven and pour the batter into the dishes. Arrange the strawberries and blueberries on top.

7. Bake for 15 to 20 minutes, until the tops of the pancakes are golden.

8. Remove from the oven and run a rubber spatula or knife around the edges. Slide the pancakes onto serving plates and sprinkle with powdered sugar, if desired. Cut into wedges and serve immediately.

PER SERVING: Calories: 258; Total fat: 9g; Total carbs: 38g; Fiber: 3g; Sugar: 15g; Protein: 8g; Sodium: 89mg

Mixed-Berry Cornmeal Muffins

NUT-FREE, SOY-FREE

MAKES 12 MUFFINS • PREP TIME: 5 MINUTES • COOK TIME: 20 MINUTES

Making muffins at home is not as challenging and time-consuming as you might think, and you'll have some leftovers to enjoy for breakfast or as a snack for a few days. Very little sugar is added to these moist and cakey muffins, because they are bursting with the naturally sweet goodness of antioxidant-rich fresh berries. Dark chocolate chips are optional, but they do add texture and depth to the flavor.

Oil or nonstick cooking spray, for greasing the pan

1½ cups all-purpose flour

¾ cup yellow cornmeal

⅓ cup sugar

4 teaspoons baking powder

¼ teaspoon salt

¾ cup blueberries

½ cup raspberries or blackberries

⅓ cup dark chocolate chips (optional)

1 large egg

1 cup milk

¼ cup extra-virgin olive oil

1½ teaspoons vanilla extract

1. Preheat the oven to 400°F.

2. Grease the cups of a muffin tin.

3. In a large bowl, whisk together the flour, cornmeal, sugar, baking powder, and salt. Stir in the berries and chocolate chips, if using, and make a well in the center of the mixture.

4. In a small bowl, lightly beat the egg. Add the milk, olive oil, and vanilla extract, and whisk until well combined.

5. Add the egg mixture into the well in the flour mixture and stir gently, until just combined.

6. Spoon the mixture evenly into the prepared muffin cups.

7. Bake for 15 to 20 minutes, or until a cake tester or toothpick inserted into the middle of each muffin comes out clean.

8. Let the muffins sit for a few minutes and then transfer to a wire rack to cool slightly. Serve warm or at room temperature.

TECHNIQUE TIP: For moist, light, and airy muffins, take care not to over-mix. Stir the wet ingredients into the dry ingredients until everything is just combined.

PER SERVING: Calories: 149; Total fat: 6g; Total carbs: 23g; Fiber: 1g; Sugar: 8g; Protein: 3g; Sodium: 70mg

Falafel Hummus Bowls 56

Chapter 3

SALADS AND BOWLS

This chapter challenges the notion that salads are simply side dishes that must be endured to satisfy that essential dose of vegetables. There are classics here that work well as meal accompaniments, as well as more substantial options that are sufficiently well-balanced with essential nutrients and complete proteins to serve as a meal on their own; the bowls are made for just that purpose. No matter your needs, you will find plenty of refreshing, vibrant, and easy salads that you can serve for lunch, dinner, as meal accompaniments, and even a few that work for dessert.

Creamy Caesar Salad
with Toasted Nuts

GLUTEN-FREE, SOY-FREE
SERVES 4 ● PREP TIME: 10 MINUTES ● COOK TIME: 5 MINUTES

I've made countless vegetarian Caesar salads over the years, but this is my ever-popular classic version. The dressing is blissfully creamy and tangy and the salad is so rich and satisfying, you won't miss the bacon. No croutons are required, and I've added lightly toasted nuts for additional protein and crunchy contrast. This salad is an ideal light summer meal, especially if you serve it up with some crusty bread on the side, but it remains a popular choice no matter the occasion or time of year.

For the dressing

⅓ cup mayonnaise

2½ tablespoons red wine vinegar

2 garlic cloves, minced

2 teaspoons Dijon mustard

Freshly ground black pepper

¼ to ⅓ cup extra-virgin olive oil

2 tablespoons lemon juice (optional)

¾ cup fresh grated Parmesan cheese, divided

For the salad

½ cup slivered almonds

½ cup walnut pieces

1 head romaine lettuce

To make the dressing

1. In a small bowl, whisk together the mayonnaise, red wine vinegar, garlic, mustard, and black pepper.

2. Drizzle in the olive oil, add the lemon juice, if using, and ½ cup of the grated Parmesan. Whisk to combine.

To make the salad

1. In a small skillet, dry-toast the nuts over medium-low heat for 5 minutes, stirring often, until they darken a few shades.

2. Tear the lettuce into pieces over a large bowl.

3. Toss the lettuce with the dressing, and sprinkle with the remaining ¼ cup of the grated Parmesan, more black pepper, if desired, and toasted nuts.

4. Serve immediately.

SUBSTITUTION TIP: Bags of prewashed mixed greens can be used instead of the romaine.

PER SERVING: Calories: 523; Total fat: 50g; Total carbs: 9g; Fiber: 4g; Sugar: 2g; Protein: 13g; Sodium: 366mg

Creamy Avocado, Carrot, and Kale Slaw with Chickpeas

VEGAN, GLUTEN-FREE, DAIRY-FREE, NUT-FREE, OIL-FREE, SOY-FREE
SERVES 4 ● PREP TIME: 10 MINUTES

A refreshing twist on classic coleslaw, shredded carrots and kale are dressed up with a dairy-free creamy and tangy dressing and topped with plump chickpeas. It's a powerhouse of nutrition, with plenty of protein from the chickpeas, iron-rich kale and beta-carotene–loaded carrots.

For the dressing

1 avocado, pitted and peeled

3 tablespoons lemon juice

2 tablespoons apple cider vinegar

2 teaspoons Dijon mustard

2 tablespoons fresh chives
(or 2 teaspoons dried chives)

½ teaspoon ground cumin

2 teaspoons brown sugar

1 teaspoon salt

Freshly ground black pepper

For the salad

1 (14-ounce) can chickpeas

1 bunch fresh kale

2 cups shredded carrot

To make the dressing

In a food processor, pulse together the avocado, lemon juice, apple cider vinegar, mustard, chives, cumin, brown sugar, salt, and pepper until creamy and well blended.

To make the salad

1. Drain and rinse the chickpeas and transfer to a large bowl.

2. Cut and discard the kale stalks and roughly chop the leaves into thin strips. Transfer to the bowl, along with the carrot.

3. Pour the dressing over the salad, toss well to coat, and serve.

PER SERVING: Calories: 242; Total fat: 9g; Total carbs: 35g; Fiber: 10g; Sugar: 8g; Protein: 9g; Sodium: 688mg

Avocado Greek Salad

GLUTEN-FREE, NUT-FREE, SOY-FREE
SERVES 4 TO 6 • PREP TIME: 10 MINUTES

A good Greek salad needs little adornment, but this twist on a classic features refreshing chunks of nutrient-rich creamy avocado. Vibrant and bursting with fresh flavors, each bite is a medley of textures and tastes. This salad is substantial enough to serve as a meal by itself. For more variety and contrast, add a mix of bell peppers, such as orange and yellow, toss in some chopped radicchio, and use a selection of mixed greens in place of the leaf lettuce.

For the dressing

⅓ cup extra-virgin olive oil

⅓ cup red wine vinegar

3 tablespoons lemon juice

1 teaspoon dried thyme

1 teaspoon dried basil

For the salad

3 cups leaf lettuce, torn into bite-size pieces

1 small red onion, cut into ½-inch-thick slices and halved

2 baby cucumbers, sliced into ½-inch-thick rounds

1 red bell pepper, cut into 1-inch strips

2 cups cherry tomatoes, halved

1 cup pitted Kalamata olives, halved

2 avocados, pitted, peeled, and coarsely chopped

1 to 1½ cups feta cheese, cut into ½-inch chunks

To make the dressing

In a small bowl, whisk together the olive oil, red wine vinegar, lemon juice, thyme, and basil.

To make the salad

1. In a large bowl, toss together the lettuce, onion, cucumbers, bell pepper, tomatoes, and olives.

2. Add the avocados to the bowl.

continued ➤

3. Pour the dressing over the salad and toss to coat.

4. To serve, transfer to serving plates and top with the feta cheese.

SERVING TIP: Omit the avocado to make a classic-style Greek salad.

PER SERVING: Calories: 476; Total fat: 40g; Total carbs: 26g; Fiber: 11g; Sugar: 10g; Protein: 9g; Sodium: 655mg

Tomato and Couscous Parsley Salad with Marinated Feta

NUT-FREE, SOY-FREE
SERVES 4 • PREP TIME: 15 MINUTES • COOK TIME: 5 MINUTES

In this fresh and colorful Middle Eastern–style salad that is based on tabbouleh, quick-cooking couscous is mixed with lots of fresh parsley, red peppers, and cherry tomatoes. The crowning touch is the small chunks of marinated feta cheese that add a complementary punch to a salad that is already bursting with flavor. You may wish to include an assortment of bell peppers, such as orange and yellow, for added color.

½ cup water

⅓ cup couscous

1 cup feta cheese, cubed

5 tablespoons extra-virgin olive oil, divided

1½ teaspoons za'atar

⅔ teaspoon ground coriander

½ teaspoon ground cumin

½ teaspoon chili powder

1 bunch fresh parsley, finely chopped

3 or 4 green onions, white and green parts, finely sliced

1 red bell pepper, seeded and diced

2 cups cherry tomatoes, halved or quartered

2 or 3 tablespoons lemon juice

½ teaspoon sea salt

Freshly ground black pepper

1. Bring the water to a boil in a small saucepan. Stir in the couscous, cover, remove from the heat, and let rest for at least 5 minutes.

2. Meanwhile, in a small bowl, gently toss the feta cheese with 1½ tablespoons of the olive oil, za'atar, coriander, cumin, and chili powder. Set aside to marinate while you prepare the salad, tossing occasionally.

3. In a large bowl, toss together the parsley, green onions, bell pepper, and cherry tomatoes.

4. Fluff the couscous with a fork and stir into the salad.

5. Add the lemon juice and remaining 3½ tablespoons of the olive oil and toss well to coat the vegetables. Season with salt and pepper.

continued ➤

6. To serve, divide the salad onto serving plates and top with some of the pieces of marinated feta cheese.

SUBSTITUTION TIP: Za'atar is a highly aromatic, zesty, and salty Middle Eastern spice blend of toasted sesame seeds, dried thyme, marjoram, and sumac. Premade blends can be found at specialty stores and most large supermarkets. If you can't find it, sprinkle in some dried Italian herb seasoning instead.

PER SERVING: Calories: 326; Total fat: 24g; Total carbs: 22g; Fiber: 4g; Sugar: 7g; Protein: 8g; Sodium: 573mg

Greek Salad Dressed with Hummus

GLUTEN-FREE, NUT-FREE, SOY-FREE
SERVES 4 • PREP TIME: 10 MINUTES

Greek salad never gets boring, but why not dress it up further? Not only does creamy hummus provide additional protein, but it's also a good way to use leftover hummus.

For the dressing

1½ cups prepared hummus
(see page 149)

⅓ cup red wine vinegar

½ cup extra-virgin olive oil

2 tablespoons white vinegar

3 tablespoons lemon juice

For the salad

3 cups leaf lettuce, torn into bite-size pieces

1 red bell pepper, seeded and cut into 1-inch strips

1 small red onion, cut into ½-inch-thick slices, and halved

2 small baby cucumbers, sliced into ½-inch-thick rounds

2 cups cherry tomatoes, halved

1 to 1½ cups feta cheese, crumbled and divided

1 cup pitted black or Kalamata olives, halved

To make the dressing

In a medium bowl, whisk together the hummus, red wine vinegar, olive oil, white vinegar, and lemon juice. If the dressing seems too thick, whisk in more oil or vinegar.

To make the salad

1. In a large bowl, toss together the lettuce, bell pepper, onion, cucumbers, tomatoes, 1 cup of the feta cheese, and olives.

2. To serve, arrange the salad onto plates, spoon some of the dressing over each serving, and top with remaining ½ cup of the feta.

PER SERVING: Calories: 499; Total fat: 41g; Total carbs: 26g; Fiber: 8g; Sugar: 9g; Protein: 12g; Sodium: 859mg

Summer Chickpea Salad with Olives and Feta

GLUTEN-FREE, NUT-FREE, SOY-FREE
SERVES 4 ● PREP TIME: 10 MINUTES

This vibrant and refreshing salad does not require any cooking at all, so it's especially ideal for those hot summer months when you don't even want to turn on the stove. Loaded with flavor and color and packed with protein, it's a great dish to enjoy outside and can easily be doubled or even tripled to serve larger groups of people.

For the dressing

3 tablespoons lemon juice

3 tablespoons extra-virgin olive oil

½ teaspoon dried mint

½ teaspoon sea salt

Freshly ground black pepper

For the salad

1 (14-ounce) can chickpeas

1 cup cherry or grape tomatoes, halved

1 red bell pepper, seeded and chopped

1 jalapeño pepper, seeded and chopped (optional)

½ cup pitted black or Kalamata olives, sliced

1 cup feta cheese, crumbled

To make the dressing

Whisk together the lemon juice, olive oil, mint, salt, and pepper.

To make the salad

1. Drain and rinse the chickpeas and transfer to a small bowl.

2. Add the tomatoes, bell pepper, jalapeño pepper, if using, olives, and feta cheese.

3. Pour dressing over the salad and gently toss.

4. Serve cold or at room temperature.

PER SERVING: Calories: 306; Total fat: 20g; Total carbs: 24g; Fiber: 6g; Sugar: 7g; Protein: 11g; Sodium: 706mg

Lazy Summer Cottage Cheese and Fruit Salad

GLUTEN-FREE, NUT-FREE, OIL-FREE, SOY-FREE
SERVES 4 ● PREP TIME: 10 MINUTES

This is a perfect lunch or dinner on those sweltering hot days when cooking seems unthinkable. Mild dry curd cottage cheese, also called dry-pressed cottage cheese or farmer's cheese, is loaded with protein and calcium and provides the creamy contrast to a colorful array of fruits and berries in this refreshing no-cook summer salad. Use your own favorite medley of fresh fruits like peaches, apricots, melons, or raspberries as you prefer.

1 (16-ounce) package, or 3 cups, dry curd cottage cheese, crumbled

1 cup green grapes, halved

1 cup blueberries

1 cup strawberries, halved or quartered

1 cup fresh cherries, pitted

3 kiwi fruits, peeled and quartered

2 apples, cored and chopped

Gently toss the ingredients together in a large bowl. Serve at room temperature or cold.

SUBSTITUTION TIP: Regular cottage cheese can be substituted for dry curd cottage cheese by draining it through a cheesecloth or fine-mesh strainer until dry. Queso fresco is very similar to dry curd cottage cheese and may also be substituted.

PER SERVING: Calories: 238; Total fat: 1g; Total carbs: 46g; Fiber: 7g; Sugar: 29g; Protein: 16g; Sodium: 15mg

Roasted-Fruit Salad with Creamy Goat Cheese Dressing

GLUTEN-FREE, SOY-FREE
SERVES 4 TO 6 • PREP TIME: 15 MINUTES • COOK TIME: 10 MINUTES

Roasted sweet peaches and plums make a wonderful addition to late-summer green salads, and a creamy, tangy goat cheese and honey dressing makes this salad an extraordinary and flavorful light patio meal, especially served with some fresh crusty bread. You can also use the dressing for any number of salads or vegetables throughout the year. You might even be tempted to eat it by itself!

For the dressing

1 (4-ounce) package soft unripened goat cheese, divided

2 teaspoons honey

1½ tablespoons extra-virgin olive oil

2 tablespoons lemon juice

1 teaspoon white wine vinegar

Pinch salt

Freshly ground black pepper

For the salad

Oil or nonstick cooking spray, for greasing the pan

2 firm ripe peaches, pitted and cut into wedges

2 red or black plums, pitted and cut into wedges

6 cups salad greens

½ cup fresh basil, chopped

½ cup walnuts or pecans, chopped

To make the dressing

Whisk together half of the goat cheese with the honey, olive oil, lemon juice, white wine vinegar, salt, and pepper until smooth.

To make the salad

1. Preheat the oven to broil and set the rack to the top level. Lightly grease a broiling pan or oven-safe sheet pan with oil and arrange the fruit wedges on the pan.

2. Broil for 5 to 8 minutes, until the fruit just begins to dry out and starts to brown slightly on the edges.

3. Arrange the salad greens and basil on a serving plate and scatter the walnuts or pecans over top.

4. Arrange the wedges of roasted fruit on top.

5. Drizzle the dressing over the salad, top with the remaining goat cheese, and serve.

SUBSTITUTION TIP: Use half of an 8-ounce cream cheese brick or half of an 8-ounce container of cream cheese spread in place of the goat cheese.

PER SERVING: Calories: 291; Total fat: 21g; Total carbs: 21g; Fiber: 5g; Sugar: 14g; Protein: 10g; Sodium: 242mg

Couscous with Harissa Chickpeas

VEGAN, DAIRY-FREE, NUT-FREE, SOY-FREE
SERVES 2 • PREP TIME: 5 MINUTES • COOK TIME: 10 MINUTES

If you know how to boil water, you know how to make couscous, which is why this no-fuss and quick-cooking tiny pasta should be a staple in the pantry of anyone who needs to make a meal on short notice.

For the salad

½ cup vegetable stock

1 teaspoon extra-virgin olive oil

½ cup couscous (semolina or whole-wheat)

¼ teaspoon salt

1 (14-ounce) can chickpeas, drained and rinsed

For the dressing

1 tablespoon extra-virgin olive oil

1 tablespoon lemon juice

1 teaspoon minced garlic

½ teaspoon dried red chili flakes

½ teaspoon ground cumin

¼ teaspoon dried mint

¼ teaspoon salt

1. Bring the vegetable stock and olive oil to a boil in a medium saucepan.

2. Remove the saucepan from the heat and stir in the couscous and salt.

3. Cover the saucepan and let sit for 10 minutes. If the couscous is still a little crunchy, let sit, covered, for a few more minutes.

4. Gently fluff the couscous with a fork.

5. While the couscous is cooking, make the dressing by whisking together the olive oil, lemon juice, garlic, red chili flakes, cumin, mint, and salt in a medium bowl.

6. Add the chickpeas to the dressing and stir to coat the chickpeas.

7. Divide the couscous onto two plates and spoon the chickpeas over top.

PER SERVING: Calories: 450; Total fat: 13g; Total carbs: 68g; Fiber: 12g; Sugar: 7g; Protein: 17g; Sodium: 791mg

Creamy Herbed Potato and Green Pea Salad

GLUTEN-FREE, DAIRY-FREE, NUT-FREE, SOY-FREE
SERVES 4 ● PREP TIME: 10 MINUTES ● COOK TIME: 20 MINUTES

This simple salad of baby potatoes, green peas, and fresh herbs tossed in a creamy mayonnaise and Dijon mustard dressing is just the thing to give you a taste of summer comfort food. It's especially delicious if you have fresh, tender garden peas, although frozen peas will certainly do. Either way, this is a lovely salad that can be enjoyed on the patio.

For the dressing

½ cup mayonnaise

1 teaspoon Dijon mustard (coarse grain if available)

2 tablespoons lemon juice

½ teaspoon salt

½ teaspoon freshly ground black pepper

For the salad

1½ pounds baby potatoes, unpeeled

1 cup green peas, frozen or fresh

1½ tablespoons fresh parsley, finely chopped

1 tablespoon fresh mint, finely chopped

1 tablespoon fresh chives, finely chopped (optional)

1 tablespoon fresh dill (optional)

To make the dressing

Whisk together the mayonnaise, mustard, lemon juice, salt, and pepper in a small bowl until smooth.

To make the salad

1. Boil the potatoes in a large saucepan of water for 20 minutes, until tender.

2. While the potatoes are cooking, boil the green peas in a small saucepan of water for 5 minutes. Drain the peas and set aside.

3. When the potatoes have cooked, drain them and let cool for a few minutes.

continued ➤

4. Cut the potatoes into halves or bite-size pieces and transfer to a medium bowl.

5. Add the green peas, parsley, and mint.

6. Pour the dressing over the salad and gently toss.

7. Serve warm, cold, or at room temperature, and sprinkle servings with fresh chives and dill, if using.

SUBSTITUTION TIP: Dried mint, chives, or dill may be used instead of fresh by substituting 1 teaspoon of dried herbs for each tablespoon of fresh.

PER SERVING: Calories: 301; Total fat: 20g; Total carbs: 25g; Fiber: 6g; Sugar: 1g; Protein: 6g; Sodium: 555mg

Potato Salad with a Harissa-Style Dressing

VEGAN, GLUTEN-FREE, DAIRY-FREE, NUT-FREE, SOY-FREE
SERVES 6 • PREP TIME: 10 MINUTES • COOK TIME: 15 MINUTES

You don't need to find harissa in a store to make this colorful and easy potato salad. Instead, a red pepper and a few spices (that you can adjust to your taste) are quickly fried and blended to make an easy dressing that will appeal to anyone who likes a little kick in their meals. This salad is delicious served warm straight from the kitchen but tastes just as good if refrigerated and served cold.

For the salad

1 pound fingerling or baby potatoes (assorted colors, if available)

3 or 4 green onions, white and green parts, sliced

¼ cup fresh mint leaves, finely chopped

¼ cup fresh cilantro, finely chopped

1 teaspoon salt

For the dressing

2 tablespoons extra-virgin olive oil

1 red bell pepper, seeded and chopped

2 fresh red chiles, seeded and minced (optional)

1 teaspoon ground coriander

1 teaspoon ground cumin

1 teaspoon ground turmeric (optional)

¼ teaspoon cayenne pepper (optional)

2 tablespoons lime juice

To make the salad

1. Cut the potatoes into 1-inch pieces and place in a medium saucepan. Cover with cold water.

2. Bring to a boil, reduce the heat to medium-high, and simmer uncovered for 10 to 12 minutes, until the potatoes are fork tender but still firm.

3. Drain the potatoes and transfer to a medium bowl. Add the green onions, mint, cilantro, and salt.

continued ➤

To make the dressing

1. While the potatoes are cooking, heat the olive oil in a large skillet over medium-high heat.

2. When the oil is hot, add the red bell pepper and chiles, if using. Fry for a few minutes, until the pepper is seared and the skin blistered.

3. Add the coriander, cumin, turmeric, and cayenne, if using. Stir for 1 minute.

4. Transfer the pepper mixture to a blender or food processor and add the lime juice. Process into a smooth paste and add to the potatoes. Toss well to coat.

5. Serve right away or refrigerate to serve later.

TECHNIQUE TIP: Fresh mint, cilantro, and other herbs can be quickly chopped by bunching the herbs into a small ball before cutting with a sharp knife.

PER SERVING: Calories: 108; Total fat: 5g; Total carbs: 16g; Fiber: 3g; Sugar: 2g; Protein: 2g; Sodium: 396mg

Black Bean Salsa with Tortilla Chips

GLUTEN-FREE, NUT-FREE, SOY-FREE
SERVES 4 ● PREP TIME: 10 MINUTES

Dressing up tortilla chips with a quick and easy, Mexican-inspired, tart and creamy salsa is not only a satisfying meal but also a good choice for snack nights. There is no shame in even having salsa for dinner when you load it up with protein-rich black beans and feta cheese. This salsa is a vibrant flavor fest, with olives, sun-dried tomatoes, cilantro, and lime.

1 (14-ounce) can black beans

3 green onions, white and green parts, thinly sliced

1 jalapeño pepper, seeded and chopped

⅔ cup pitted black or Kalamata olives, halved

¾ cup feta cheese, crumbled

6 sun-dried tomatoes, chopped

2 teaspoons honey

⅓ cup fresh cilantro, finely chopped

3 tablespoons lime juice

1 (5-ounce) bag corn tortilla chips

1. Drain and rinse the black beans and transfer to a medium bowl.

2. Add the green onions, jalapeño pepper, olives, feta cheese, sun-dried tomatoes, honey, cilantro, and lime juice to the bowl, and toss to combine.

3. Let the mixture sit for 5 to 10 minutes to allow the flavors to blend.

4. To serve, line serving plates with tortilla chips and scoop some salsa over top.

SERVING TIP: Serve with a side salad to balance out the meal.

PER SERVING: Calories: 430; Total fat: 17g; Total carbs: 56g; Fiber: 13g; Sugar: 8g; Protein: 16g; Sodium: 713mg

Tex-Mex Burrito Bowls

GLUTEN-FREE, NUT-FREE, OIL-FREE, SOY-FREE
SERVES 4 TO 6 ● PREP TIME: 10 MINUTES

These colorful bowls have all the classic tastes of Tex-Mex food combined into an easy complete meal of refried beans, sour cream, salsa, and guacamole, all served over tortilla chips that can be used to scoop up the toppings. While you can find many good brands of refried beans and salsa in supermarkets, store-bought guacamole lacks the vibrancy and flavor of guacamole made fresh at home, which is why you'll find a recipe for a crowd-pleasing homemade guacamole here. Speaking of crowds, everything in these bowls can instead be served on a platter to share.

For the guacamole

2 ripe avocados, pitted and peeled

2 tomatoes, seeded and finely chopped

2 shallots, finely chopped

2 green onions, white and green parts, finely sliced

2 teaspoons minced garlic

2 jalapeño peppers, seeded and finely chopped

¼ teaspoon ground cumin

¼ teaspoon chili powder

2 tablespoons fresh cilantro, chopped

Salt

Freshly ground black pepper

For the bowls

1 (5-ounce) bag corn tortilla chips

1 (14-ounce) can refried beans or prepared refried beans (see page 155)

1 (8.5-ounce) container sour cream

1 cup jarred or prepared salsa (see page 53)

To make the guacamole

1. In a medium-large bowl, mash the avocado with a potato masher or fork.

2. Add the tomatoes, shallots, green onions, garlic, jalapeño peppers, cumin, chili powder, and cilantro. Mash well to combine and season with salt and pepper.

To make the bowls

To serve, arrange the tortilla chips in 4 to 6 serving dishes. Top with guacamole, refried beans, sour cream, and salsa.

> **SHOPPING TIP:** To choose a ripe avocado, squeeze it gently. It should yield to firm, gentle pressure but should not feel mushy.

> **TECHNIQUE TIP:** To seed a tomato, cut into quarters. Using a sharp knife, cut the seeds and white core away from the tomato flesh and discard.

PER SERVING: Calories: 582; Total fat: 35g; Total carbs: 58g; Fiber: 16g; Sugar: 5g; Protein: 14g; Sodium: 1054mg

Falafel Hummus Bowls

VEGAN, GLUTEN-FREE, DAIRY-FREE, NUT-FREE, SOY-FREE
SERVES 4 TO 6 • PREP TIME: 10 MINUTES • COOK TIME: 20 MINUTES

Chickpeas are a treasured legume, and even those who claim they don't like beans enjoy them. You get a double dose of protein-rich chickpea goodness here, because in addition to the crispy baked falafel, the bowl is adorned with a healthy dose of creamy hummus. For additional nutrients and balanced protein, nutty quinoa provides a base and the bowl is also lined with leafy greens.

For the falafel

2 (14-ounce) cans chickpeas

1 small onion, chopped

1 tablespoon minced garlic

1 teaspoon ground cumin

1½ teaspoons ground coriander

1 teaspoon baking powder

½ cup fresh parsley, roughly chopped

2 teaspoons sesame oil

1 teaspoon salt

For the bowls

⅔ cup quinoa, well-rinsed

1⅓ cups water

1 (5-ounce) bag mixed greens

1½ cups prepared hummus
(see page 149)

To make the falafel

1. Preheat the oven to 375° and line a baking sheet with parchment paper.

2. Drain and rinse the chickpeas and transfer to a food processor.

3. Add the onion, garlic, cumin, coriander, baking powder, parsley, sesame oil, and salt. Process until well combined. The mixture should be fairly dry, but moist enough to shape into small patties. Add more oil or a bit of flour if necessary.

4. Shape the mixture into 12 2-inch-round patties and place on the prepared baking sheet.

5. Bake for 20 minutes or until golden brown, turning the falafel over partway through the baking time.

To make the bowls

1. While the falafel is baking, in a medium saucepan, combine the quinoa and the water. Bring to a boil, reduce the heat to medium-low, cover, and simmer until the liquid is absorbed, about 15 minutes.

2. Remove the quinoa from the heat, let sit for a few minutes, and then fluff with a fork.

3. To serve, arrange some of the mixed greens over the bottom of 4 to 6 serving dishes. Spoon quinoa into one side of each dish, top with 2 or 3 falafels, and scoop some hummus over top.

SERVING TIP: Cut two pita breads into triangles and place on a baking sheet lined with parchment paper. Brush with olive oil and toast in a preheated 350°F oven for 3 to 5 minutes, until golden brown. Arrange the pitas along the side of the bowls.

PER SERVING: Calories: 450; Total fat: 13g; Total carbs: 65g; Fiber: 16g; Sugar: 7g; Protein: 21g; Sodium: 852mg

Stuffed Portobellos with Spinach, Sun-Dried Tomatoes, and Black Olives

VEGAN, GLUTEN-FREE, DAIRY-FREE, NUT-FREE, SOY-FREE
SERVES 4 ● PREP TIME: 10 MINUTES ● COOK TIME: 20 MINUTES

Much more than a side, these gorgeous, succulent stuffed mushrooms can easily be served as a salad, especially when dished up over a bed of mixed greens splashed with some fresh lemon juice and seasoned with some salt and freshly ground black pepper. To make the meal even more substantial, include some brown rice to complement the earthy mushrooms and add additional protein to the meal.

1½ tablespoons extra-virgin olive oil, divided, plus more for greasing

2 teaspoons balsamic vinegar

6 medium portobello mushrooms

2 tablespoons chickpea flour

½ cup water

2 tablespoons nutritional yeast

1 shallot or small onion, finely chopped

1 or 2 green chiles, seeded and minced (optional)

6 cups baby spinach, roughly chopped

4 to 6 sun-dried tomatoes, finely chopped

4 tablespoons pitted black or Kalamata olives, finely chopped

½ teaspoon salt

1. Preheat the oven to 450°F. Line a baking sheet with aluminum foil and lightly grease with olive oil.

2. In a small bowl, whisk together the olive oil and balsamic vinegar.

3. Wipe the mushrooms clean with a damp cloth. Remove the stems and finely chop. Set aside.

4. Gently hollow out the middle of each mushroom cap, leaving some of the mushroom interior so they retain their shape and some of their meatiness. Transfer the mushroom caps to the prepared baking sheet, hollow side down, and brush with the oil-and-vinegar mixture.

5. Bake the mushrooms for 5 minutes, until the mushrooms just begin to release their juices. Remove from the oven and wipe any excess juice from the baking sheet. Reduce the oven heat to 400°F.

6. In another small bowl, whisk together the chickpea flour and water and let sit for 5 minutes, then whisk in the nutritional yeast.

7. In a large frying pan, heat the remaining ½ tablespoon of oil over medium heat. Stir in the shallot, chiles, if using, and mushroom stems, and sauté for 3 to 5 minutes to soften.

8. Add the spinach a few handfuls at a time and stir until wilted. Stir the chickpea flour mixture into the pan, along with the sun-dried tomatoes, olives, and salt. Cook for another few minutes, stirring frequently.

9. Flip the mushroom caps over on the baking pan. Evenly distribute the filling from the pan into the hollows of the mushrooms and press it down with the back of a small spoon.

10. Bake the mushrooms for 5 to 7 minutes, until the filling starts to brown. Place the pan under the broiler for a few more minutes to brown further.

11. Remove from the oven and serve.

SUBSTITUTION TIPS: Replace the chiles with ¼ to ½ teaspoon red pepper flakes. If you don't have chickpea flour, use 4 tablespoons all-purpose flour instead. Nutritional yeast provides protein and a "cheesy" flavor but may be replaced with bread crumbs or cornmeal.

PER SERVING: Calories: 130; Total fat: 5g; Total carbs: 14g; Fiber: 5g; Sugar: 1g; Protein: 11g; Sodium: 446mg

Lemony Pasta with Broccoli and Chickpeas 64

Chapter 4

PASTAS AND NOODLES

Pasta is a staple pantry essential. Easy to cook and filling, it comes in all shapes and sizes, with a vast range of ways to showcase it. The recipes in this chapter are much more than just a combination of prepre-pared sauces and cooked noodles, yet they all come together quickly for a meal that you can sit down to enjoy in 30 minutes or less. These recipes can easily be adjusted to make them gluten-free, too. Supermarkets offer an array of pastas that have no gluten, such as brown rice and quinoa, and in most cases it's just a matter of a simple swap.

Pasta with Sun-Dried Tomato Sauce

NUT-FREE, SOY-FREE
SERVES 4 • PREP TIME: 5 MINUTES • COOK TIME: 10 MINUTES

Store-bought pasta sauces are a go-to for many cooks in a hurry, and I used to rely on them myself when I first started cooking. That is, until I learned just how easy and quick they are to make at home, especially when you don't need to simmer the sauce. Sun-dried tomatoes have an intense sweet-and-tart flavor that elevates this pasta sauce above ordinary tomato sauces.

3 cups dried fusilli or rotini pasta

1 large tomato, chopped

⅔ cup sun-dried tomatoes, chopped

2 cloves garlic, coarsely chopped

½ cup fresh parsley, coarsely chopped

½ cup fresh grated Parmesan cheese

¼ cup balsamic vinegar

⅓ cup extra-virgin olive oil

1. Bring a large pot of salted water to a boil. Add the pasta and cook according to package instructions.

2. While the pasta is cooking, combine the tomato, sun-dried tomatoes, garlic, parsley, Parmesan cheese, balsamic vinegar, and olive oil in a blender. Blend until smooth.

3. Drain the pasta and transfer to serving plates.

4. Ladle the sauce over the pasta and serve hot.

SUBSTITUTION TIPS: Red wine vinegar may be used instead of balsamic vinegar for a milder flavor. Substitute 1 tablespoon of minced garlic for the fresh cloves.

PER SERVING: Calories: 419; Total fat: 22g; Total carbs: 48g; Fiber: 7g; Sugar: 5g; Protein: 14g; Sodium: 324mg

Zesty Green Pea and Jalapeño Pesto Pasta

VEGAN, DAIRY-FREE, NUT-FREE, SOY-FREE
SERVES 4 ● PREP TIME: 5 MINUTES ● COOK TIME: 10 MINUTES

This is one of my favorite pasta dishes, loaded with flavor from a zesty and lemony pesto made from peas, fresh herbs, sun-dried tomatoes, and a jalapeño for a little added kick. It takes little time to prepare and cook and is delicious served either hot from the stove or cold as a salad.

3 cups dried fusilli or rotini pasta

1¼ cups fresh or defrosted frozen green peas, divided

4 sun-dried tomatoes, chopped

1 cup fresh basil leaves, chopped

¾ cup fresh mint leaves, chopped

1 small onion, chopped

2 cloves garlic, coarsely chopped

1 jalapeño pepper, seeded and chopped

3 tablespoons lemon juice

¼ teaspoon salt

¼ teaspoon freshly ground black pepper

3 tablespoons extra-virgin olive oil

1. Bring a large pot of salted water to a boil. Add the pasta and cook according to package instructions.

2. Two minutes before the pasta is finished cooking, toss in 1 cup of the peas.

3. While the pasta is cooking, combine the remaining ¼ cup of the peas with the sun-dried tomatoes, basil, mint, onion, garlic, jalapeño pepper, lemon juice, salt, pepper, and olive oil in a blender.

4. Blend until smooth. Add another tablespoon of olive oil if the mixture is too thick to process.

5. Drain the pasta and peas and toss with the pesto.

6. Serve hot or warm, or cold as a salad.

PER SERVING: Calories: 345; Total fat: 13g; Total carbs: 52g; Fiber: 10g; Sugar: 5g; Protein: 11g; Sodium: 200mg

Lemony Pasta with Broccoli and Chickpeas

VEGAN, DAIRY-FREE, NUT-FREE, SOY-FREE
SERVES 6 ● PREP TIME: 5 MINUTES ● COOK TIME: 10 MINUTES

This is such a simple, nourishing, and attractive meal that you'll find yourself making it again and again. Broccoli is a well-known source of fiber and many vitamins and minerals, including iron and potassium. Add chickpeas for protein, and you have a complete meal. Try tossing in a few pinches of dried red chili flakes for a bit of zest, or garnish with grated Parmesan cheese.

3 cups dried fusilli or rotini pasta

3 cups broccoli florets

1 (14-ounce) can chickpeas, drained and rinsed

⅓ cup sun-dried tomatoes, chopped

2 tablespoons extra-virgin olive oil

½ tablespoon minced garlic

½ teaspoon paprika

3 tablespoons lemon juice

1 teaspoon salt

1. Bring a large pot of salted water to a boil. Add the pasta and cook according to package instructions.

2. In the last 4 minutes of the pasta cooking time, add the broccoli florets.

3. Drain the pasta and broccoli and add to a large bowl.

4. Add the chickpeas, sun-dried tomatoes, olive oil, garlic, paprika, lemon juice, and salt.

5. Stir to combine and serve warm or cold.

SUBSTITUTION TIP: Instead of buying broccoli florets, use the florets and stem from a fresh head of broccoli. The stems are sweet and tender, once peeled, and have the same nutritional value as the crown. You can peel and chop the stem and add to the pasta cooking water, just as with the florets.

PER SERVING: Calories: 270; Total fat: 7g; Total carbs: 43g; Fiber: 9g; Sugar: 5g; Protein: 10g; Sodium: 469mg

Penne with Indian-Style Tomato Sauce and Mushrooms

VEGAN, DAIRY-FREE, NUT-FREE, SOY-FREE
SERVES 4 • PREP TIME: 5 MINUTES • COOK TIME: 20 MINUTES

Ginger and garam masala give this tomato pasta sauce a spicy and enticing Indian character. Ginger is one of nature's healthiest spices, providing many scientifically proven benefits, including aiding digestion and reducing inflammation. Garam masala is a hot and aromatic Indian spice blend that, like many other international ingredients, has gained attention and popularity lately and can be found in most supermarkets.

---

2 tablespoons extra-virgin olive oil

1 (8-ounce) package sliced white mushrooms

2 tablespoons minced fresh ginger

2 tablespoons minced garlic

½ tablespoon garam masala

¼ teaspoon dried red chili flakes

1 (28-ounce) can crushed or diced tomatoes

½ teaspoon salt

3 cups dried penne pasta

---

1. In a medium saucepan, heat the olive oil over medium heat.

2. When hot, add the mushrooms and sauté for 5 minutes.

3. Add the ginger, garlic, garam masala, and red chili flakes, and stir for 3 more minutes.

4. Stir in the tomatoes and salt. Bring to a boil, being careful of splattering. Lower the heat and simmer for 10 minutes.

5. While the sauce is simmering, bring a large pot of salted water to a boil. Add the pasta and cook according to package instructions.

continued ➤

6. Drain the pasta, return to the pot, and stir in the tomato sauce.

7. Serve hot.

TECHNIQUE TIP: Two inches of fresh ginger root provides an intense ginger flavor. Peel the root with a paring knife and grate the ginger with a fine cheese grater. To save time, use jarred minced ginger.

SUBSTITUTION TIP: If you don't have garam masala, combine ½ teaspoon ground cumin, ½ teaspoon ground black pepper, and ¼ teaspoon ground cinnamon to substitute.

PER SERVING: Calories: 326; Total fat: 9g; Total carbs: 52g; Fiber: 9g; Sugar: 8g; Protein: 11g; Sodium: 306mg

Teriyaki Mushrooms and Cashews with Rice Noodles

VEGAN, GLUTEN-FREE, DAIRY-FREE
SERVES 2 • PREP TIME: 5 MINUTES • COOK TIME: 20 MINUTES

You'll wonder why it's ever necessary to purchase preprepared teriyaki sauce when you see how easy it is to make. Panfrying the mushrooms at a fairly high temperature helps retain the moisture in the mushrooms until they are slightly browned on the edges and succulent and plump in texture. The mushrooms are a perfect vehicle for the sauce, and serving them over the rice noodles fills out the meal. Fried cashews add a nutty complement to the other flavors, in addition to protein and a pleasant crunch.

2 cups water

2½ ounces rice noodles

3½ tablespoons sesame oil, divided

¼ cup raw cashews, halved or coarsely chopped

1 tablespoon brown sugar

1 tablespoon tamari or soy sauce

1 tablespoon rice vinegar

½ teaspoon dried red chili flakes

1 green onion, white and green parts, finely sliced

½ tablespoon minced garlic

1 tablespoon minced fresh ginger

1 (8-ounce) package sliced white mushrooms

1. Bring the water to a boil in a medium saucepan. Stir in the rice noodles, cover, and remove from the heat. Let sit for 5 minutes, or up to 10 minutes for wider rice noodles.

2. While the noodles are resting, heat 2 tablespoons of the sesame oil in a medium nonstick pan or wok over medium-low heat. When hot, add the cashew pieces and fry, stirring frequently, for 5 to 8 minutes, until golden brown. Remove from the pan using a slotted spoon and set aside.

3. Add 1 tablespoon of the oil to the pan and stir in the brown sugar, tamari or soy sauce, rice vinegar, red chili flakes, green onion, garlic, and ginger. Stir for 1 to 2 minutes to dissolve the sugar.

continued ➤

4. Increase the heat to medium-high and add the mushrooms. Cook, stirring frequently, for 5 minutes until the mushrooms begin to brown.

5. Stir in the cashew pieces and toss to combine.

6. Drain the rice noodles, stir in the remaining ½ tablespoon of the sesame oil, and transfer to serving plates. Spoon the mushrooms and cashews over each portion and serve immediately.

INGREDIENT TIP: Rice noodles range in width from very fine (rice vermicelli) to ¼-inch wide. These mushrooms will look attractive with any width of rice noodle, but wider noodles will provide a more "toothsome" experience.

PER SERVING: Calories: 438; Total fat: 28g; Total carbs: 40g; Fiber: 3g; Sugar: 7g; Protein: 9g; Sodium: 566mg

Linguine with Pea-Basil Pesto

VEGAN, DAIRY-FREE, SOY-FREE
SERVES 4 • PREP TIME: 5 MINUTES • COOK TIME: 10 MINUTES

Sweet, tender green peas and fragrant fresh basil leaves make this simple pesto sauce a vibrant way to adorn pasta. Walnuts are rich in good fats, vitamins, and minerals, and give the pesto a thick texture to coat the pasta and a nutty flavor that enhances the peas and basil. Thick linguine noodles make a good platform for the pesto sauce, but fettuccine will work well, too.

8 ounces dried linguine

1¼ cup fresh or defrosted frozen green peas, divided

2 tablespoons extra-virgin olive oil

1 small onion, chopped

1 tablespoon minced garlic

1 jalapeño pepper, seeded and chopped

½ cup walnuts, chopped

½ cup fresh basil leaves

½ teaspoon salt

⅔ cup water

Freshly ground black pepper

1. Bring a large pot of salted water to a boil. Add the pasta and cook according to package instructions.

2. Two minutes before the pasta is finished cooking, toss in ½ cup of the peas.

3. While the pasta is cooking, heat the olive oil in a nonstick skillet over medium heat.

4. Add the onion, garlic, and jalapeño pepper, and stir for 3 to 4 minutes to soften the onion.

5. Stir in the remaining ¾ cup of the peas and the walnuts. Continue to stir for another minute.

6. Add the basil, salt, and water. Stir for a minute and then remove from the heat.

7. Transfer the contents of the skillet to a blender and process until smooth, adding more water if the pesto is too thick.

continued ➤

8. Drain the pasta and peas and rinse quickly with cold water.

9. Return the pasta to the pot and add the pesto and black pepper. Toss gently and serve hot.

LEFTOVER TIP: Place leftover pasta in a bowl, cover with plastic wrap, and refrigerate for up to 3 days. Drizzle a little olive oil into the pasta and toss again before serving.

PER SERVING: Calories: 415; Total fat: 19g; Total carbs: 50g; Fiber: 10g; Sugar: 5g; Protein: 12g; Sodium: 294mg

Greek-Inspired Macaroni and Cheese

NUT-FREE, SOY-FREE

SERVES 6 • PREP TIME: 10 MINUTES • COOK TIME: 15 MINUTES

Mac and cheese is a famous comfort food, and it's easy to add or change ingredients to suit your style. Swiss cheese, feta cheese, spinach, and olives give this mac and cheese a delicious Greek spin. This is a stovetop version, so you don't even have to turn on the oven to serve up this old classic with a twist.

1 pound dried macaroni

2 cups fresh spinach, chopped

2 tablespoons unsalted butter

1 onion, finely chopped

1 tablespoon minced garlic

2 tablespoons all-purpose flour

1 (12-ounce) can evaporated milk or 2 cups heavy cream

1 cup grated Swiss cheese

1 cup feta cheese, crumbled

1 cup pitted black or Kalamata olives, sliced or chopped

Freshly ground black pepper (optional)

1. Bring a large pot of salted water to a boil. Add the macaroni and cook until al dente, according to package instructions.

2. Add the spinach and cook for another few minutes.

3. Drain the pasta and spinach and return to the pot.

4. While the pasta is cooking, melt the butter over medium heat in a medium saucepan. Add the onion and garlic and stir for 5 minutes to soften the onion.

5. Add the flour to the pan and stir for another 2 minutes.

6. Whisk in the evaporated milk and bring to a slow boil over medium-high heat. Continue to whisk constantly for 3 to 4 minutes, until the mixture is creamy and thickened.

continued ➤

7. Add the Swiss and feta cheeses and stir for 2 to 3 minutes to melt. Turn the heat off and stir in the olives.

8. Add the cheese mixture to the pasta and spinach and stir to combine. Serve hot or warm, seasoned with freshly ground black pepper, if desired.

LEFTOVER TIP: Refrigerate leftovers in a sealed container for up to 3 days. To reheat, put the macaroni and cheese in a covered oven-safe bowl or casserole dish and stir in a few tablespoons of milk. Reheat in a 350°F oven for 10 to 20 minutes before serving.

PER SERVING: Calories: 572; Total fat: 22g; Total carbs: 70g; Fiber: 4g; Sugar: 10g; Protein: 23g; Sodium: 610mg

Spicy Mac and Ricotta Cheese with Spinach

NUT-FREE, SOY-FREE
SERVES 4 TO 6 • PREP TIME: 5 MINUTES • COOK TIME: 25 MINUTES

A good mac and cheese is one of those comfort foods that pretty much everyone enjoys. My Indian-inspired "grown-up" version heats things up and combines the earthy goodness of creamy spinach for a healthy dose of iron. Look for bags of prewashed and chopped spinach to cut down on the preparation time. The spices and spinach complement the sweet, creamy ricotta cheese, which is an excellent source of calcium and protein.

2 cups dried macaroni

2 tablespoons extra-virgin olive oil or unsalted butter

1 medium shallot or small yellow onion, finely chopped

1 (10-ounce) bag fresh spinach, chopped

1 large tomato, finely chopped

1 or 2 fresh red or green chiles, seeded and minced

½ teaspoon turmeric

⅔ teaspoon ground coriander

½ teaspoon ground cumin

¼ teaspoon cayenne pepper

1 cup firm ricotta cheese, crumbled or mashed

1 to 2 teaspoons salt

1. Bring a large pot of salted water to a boil. Stir in the macaroni and cook until al dente, according to package instructions.

2. While the pasta is cooking, heat the olive oil in a large saucepan over medium heat. Add the shallot or onion to the pan and sauté for 4 to 5 minutes, or until softened.

3. Add handfuls of the spinach, stirring frequently, until it begins to wilt.

4. Once all of the spinach has been added, stir in the tomato, chiles, turmeric, coriander, cumin, and cayenne. Simmer for 5 minutes, or until the tomato is softened and most of the liquid has evaporated.

5. Reserve 1⅔ cups of the pasta cooking liquid and drain the pasta in a strainer.

continued ➤

6. Stir the reserved pasta cooking water into the sauce and bring to a gentle simmer over medium-high heat. Stir in the cooked pasta, ricotta cheese, and salt.

7. Reduce the heat to medium-low and continue to simmer for another 5 minutes, stirring occasionally.

8. Serve immediately.

SUBSTITUTION TIP: If you can't find or don't want to fuss with fresh chiles, use ¼ to ½ teaspoons dried red chili flakes instead.

PER SERVING: Calories: 313; Total fat: 13g; Total carbs: 36g; Fiber: 4g; Sugar: 3g; Protein: 15g; Sodium: 720mg

Spinach Pesto Pasta

SOY-FREE

SERVES 4 ● PREP TIME: 5 MINUTES ● COOK TIME: 10 MINUTES

Spinach is a nutritional powerhouse, loaded with antioxidants and nutrients that may promote eye health and reduce blood pressure and cancer risk. It's definitely delicious, raw or cooked.

8 ounces dried linguine or fettuccini

¼ cup pine nuts

1 (5-ounce) bag fresh spinach leaves

2 cloves garlic, chopped

¼ cup extra-virgin olive oil

¼ cup fresh grated Parmesan cheese

½ tablespoon balsamic vinegar or red wine vinegar

½ teaspoon salt

Freshly ground black pepper (optional)

1. Bring a large pot of salted water to a boil. Add the pasta and cook according to package instructions.

2. While the pasta is cooking, toast the pine nuts in a small dry skillet over medium-low heat for 5 minutes, tossing or stirring frequently.

3. In a blender or food processor, combine the pine nuts, spinach, and garlic, and process until well chopped.

4. Pour in the olive oil and process for another half minute until blended.

5. Transfer the spinach pesto to a medium bowl and stir in the Parmesan cheese, balsamic vinegar, and salt.

6. Drain the pasta and rinse quickly with cold water.

7. Return the pasta to the pot and add the pesto. Toss gently and serve hot with freshly ground black pepper, if desired.

SUBSTITUTION TIP: Unsalted pistachios or almonds can be substituted for pine nuts. If they are already roasted, skip the second step.

PER SERVING: Calories: 398; Total fat: 21g; Total carbs: 45g; Fiber: 3g; Sugar: 2g; Protein: 12g; Sodium: 384mg

Lasagna Noodles in a Creamy Mushroom Sauce

NUT-FREE, SOY-FREE
SERVES 4 • PREP TIME: 5 MINUTES • COOK TIME: 25 MINUTES

I've been making this creamy mushroom sauce for many years, and I never tire of it. If you are a mushroom lover like myself, it's an absolutely delicious sauce to put on mashed potatoes, lightly steamed vegetables, rice, or in this case, hot fresh-cooked pasta noodles. Mushrooms are surprisingly rich in many important nutrients, including fiber, vitamin D, and protein. Pieces of cooked lasagna noodles are almost like little bowls for holding this sauce, but pasta shells will work as well.

4 tablespoons unsalted butter

2 medium onions, chopped

1 (16-ounce) package sliced white mushrooms

1 (14-ounce) can coconut milk or cream

4 tablespoons lemon juice

2 tablespoons fresh parsley, chopped

1 tablespoon all-purpose flour

½ teaspoon dry mustard powder

1 teaspoon salt

8 ounces dried lasagna noodles

Freshly ground black pepper (optional)

1. In a large saucepan or wok, melt the butter over medium heat. Add the onions and cook, stirring often, for 5 minutes to soften.

2. Raise the heat to medium-high and add the mushrooms. Cook, stirring often, for 5 minutes until lightly browned but still plump.

3. Reduce the heat to medium-low and stir in the coconut milk or cream, lemon juice, parsley, flour, dry mustard powder, and salt. Simmer without boiling for 15 minutes, stirring occasionally. If the sauce becomes too thick, stir in a little water.

4. While the sauce is simmering, break the lasagna noodles into 2- to 3-inch pieces.

5. Bring a large pot of salted water to a boil. Add the noodles and cook until al dente, according to package instructions.

6. Drain the noodles and rinse quickly with cold water. Return the noodles to the pot.

7. Remove the sauce from the heat and add to the pasta. Toss gently and serve hot, seasoned with freshly ground black pepper, if desired.

INGREDIENT TIPS: Do not substitute coconut milk from a carton for canned coconut milk, as it is much more watery. Avoid oven-ready (or no-boil) lasagna noodles for this recipe.

PER SERVING: Calories: 550; Total fat: 37g; Total carbs: 48g; Fiber: 5g; Sugar: 8g; Protein: 14g; Sodium: 591mg

Mushroom-and-Walnut Pesto Fettuccini

VEGAN, DAIRY-FREE, SOY-FREE
SERVES 4 • PREP TIME: 10 MINUTES • COOK TIME: 10 MINUTES

This is one of my favorite ways to serve fettuccini. Walnuts not only provide protein, but also are an excellent source of anti-inflammatory omega-3 essential fatty acids and are rich in antioxidants, essential vitamins, and minerals—including vitamin E, magnesium, and calcium. In this pesto, they come together with mushrooms to make a delightfully earthy and nutty sauce for the noodles. In fact, the pesto is so rich and creamy, you'd hardly guess that it's also dairy-free.

8 ounces dried fettuccini

½ cup walnut pieces

4 tablespoons extra-virgin olive oil, divided

1 tablespoon minced garlic

1 pound cremini or white mushrooms, chopped

½ cup fresh cilantro, trimmed and chopped

½ teaspoon dried red chili flakes

2 tablespoons lime juice

1 teaspoon salt

Freshly ground black pepper

1. Bring a large pot of salted water to a boil. Add the pasta and cook according to package instructions.

2. While the pasta is cooking, in a small saucepan, dry roast the walnut pieces, stirring occasionally, for 5 to 6 minutes, or until they darken a few shades. Remove from the heat.

3. Meanwhile, heat 1 tablespoon of the olive oil in a large nonstick skillet over medium-high heat. When hot, add the garlic and mushrooms to the pan and cook for 6 to 8 minutes, or until the mushrooms begin to lose their liquid and most of the liquid evaporates. Reserve about ½ cup of the cooked mushrooms for garnish.

4. In a blender, combine the roasted walnuts, cooked garlic and mushrooms, cilantro, remaining 3 tablespoons olive oil, chili flakes, lime juice, and salt. Blend to combine.

5. Reserve 1 cup of the pasta cooking liquid and drain the pasta. Rinse the pasta under cold water and return to the pot.

6. Stir in the pesto to coat the pasta and gradually add as much of the reserved cooking liquid as needed to thin the sauce to your desired consistency.

7. To serve, divide the pasta onto serving plates and top with the reserved cooked mushrooms and black pepper.

SIMPLE SWAP: Use brown rice fettuccini to complement the nutty flavor of the pesto and to make this recipe gluten-free.

PER SERVING: Calories: 459; Total fat: 26g; Total carbs: 49g; Fiber: 5g; Sugar: 4g; Protein: 13g; Sodium: 895mg

Mushroom Spaghetti Bolognese

VEGAN, DAIRY-FREE, NUT-FREE, SOY-FREE
SERVES 6 • PREP TIME: 10 MINUTES • COOK TIME: 20 MINUTES

Mushrooms minced to small pieces take the place of ground beef in this flavorful vegetarian version of the classic spaghetti Bolognese. The sauce is very thick and has very little tomato, much as you would find in Italy rather than in Italian restaurants in North America. And like in Italy, the sauce is stirred into the pasta before serving. No matter where you are, this is a favorite of vegetarians and non-vegetarians alike.

2½ tablespoons extra-virgin olive oil, divided

1½ pounds cremini mushrooms, finely chopped

1 red onion, finely chopped

1 large carrot, finely chopped

2 cloves garlic, minced

1 pound dried spaghetti

1 large tomato, finely chopped

2 tablespoons tomato paste

1¼ cups red cooking or drinking wine

2 teaspoons balsamic or red wine vinegar

2 teaspoons dried oregano

1½ teaspoons salt

1. Heat 2 tablespoons of the olive oil in a nonstick skillet over medium-high heat. Add the mushrooms, onion, carrot, and garlic and cook, stirring often, for 10 minutes or until the mushrooms are browned.

2. While the mushrooms are cooking, bring a large pot of salted water to a boil. Add the spaghetti and cook until al dente, according to package instructions.

3. Transfer the mushroom mixture from the skillet to a bowl. Return the skillet to the stove, add the remaining ½ tablespoon of olive oil, and turn the heat down to medium.

4. Add the tomato, tomato paste, cooking wine, balsamic vinegar, oregano, and salt. Cook, stirring occasionally, for 5 minutes.

5. While the sauce is cooking, reserve ½ cup of the pasta cooking water and drain the spaghetti. Rinse quickly with cold water and return to the pot.

6. Stir the mushroom mixture and the reserved pasta cooking water into the tomato sauce. Simmer for 5 more minutes, stirring often.

7. Pour the sauce into the spaghetti and stir well to coat. Serve hot or warm.

MAKE IT FASTER: Combine coarsely chopped mushrooms, onion, carrot, and garlic in a food processor and pulse until the mushrooms and vegetables resemble coarse crumbs. Be careful not to over-process.

PER SERVING: Calories: 394; Total fat: 7g; Total carbs: 63g; Fiber: 10g; Sugar: 7g; Protein: 13g; Sodium: 410mg

Cauliflower and Spinach in a Coconut-Milk Sauce over Rice Noodles

VEGAN, GLUTEN-FREE, DAIRY-FREE, NUT-FREE, SOY-FREE
SERVES 4 ● PREP TIME: 10 MINUTES ● COOK TIME: 20 MINUTES

This is one of those dishes that tastes so divine that, when sitting down to enjoy it, you would think it was complicated. But it's not! In fact, this dish of tender cauliflower, fresh spinach, and tomato simmered in a fragrant coconut-milk sauce comes together in hardly any time at all, and it's a great way to get a big helping of nourishing vegetables. It smells and tastes just as wonderful as it looks.

2½ tablespoons extra-virgin olive oil, divided

2 cups cauliflower florets

½ tablespoon minced garlic

1 jalapeño pepper, seeded and finely chopped

1 (14-ounce) can coconut-milk

1 large tomato, diced

½ teaspoon ground cumin

½ teaspoon turmeric (optional)

4 cups water

2½ ounces rice noodles

1 (5-ounce) bag fresh spinach, chopped

1 teaspoon salt

1. Heat 2 tablespoons of the olive oil in a large saucepan over medium-high heat.

2. Add the cauliflower, garlic, and jalapeño pepper, and stir for 2 minutes.

3. Pour in the coconut milk and simmer for 2 minutes.

4. Add the tomato, cumin, and turmeric, if using.

5. Reduce the heat to medium. Cover and simmer, stirring occasionally, for 5 to 10 minutes, until the sauce begins to thicken and the cauliflower is fork tender.

6. While the cauliflower and tomato are cooking, bring water to a boil in a medium saucepan. Stir in the rice noodles, cover, and remove from the heat. Let sit for 5 minutes, or up to 10 minutes for wider rice noodles.

7. Add the spinach to the cauliflower and tomato a few handfuls at a time and stir until the spinach is wilted. Simmer for another 5 minutes. Stir in the salt.

8. Drain the rice noodles, stir in the remaining ½ tablespoon of the olive oil, and transfer to 4 serving plates. Spoon the cauliflower, spinach, and tomato mixture over each portion and serve immediately.

SUBSTITUTION TIP: Two cups of prepared riced cauliflower can be used in place of cauliflower florets for a creamier sauce. Add the riced cauliflower with the tomato in step 4, instead of step 2.

PER SERVING: Calories: 386; Total fat: 31g; Total carbs: 27g; Fiber: 5g; Sugar: 6g; Protein: 6g; Sodium: 675mg

Pasta with Roasted Brussels Sprouts and Creamy Cashew Alfredo Sauce

VEGAN, GLUTEN-FREE, DAIRY-FREE
SERVES 4 • PREP TIME: 10 MINUTES • COOK TIME: 20 MINUTES

There's no butter, cream, or guilt in this easy vegan, cashew-based Alfredo sauce that you'll want to make again and again. Cashews are an especially good source of magnesium, in addition to fiber and protein. But what really makes this pasta Alfredo a centerpiece dish is the addition of brussels sprouts, roasted to sweet, golden, crispy perfection.

For the brussels sprouts

1 pound brussels sprouts, trimmed and halved

2 tablespoons extra-virgin olive oil

½ teaspoon salt

For the pasta

1½ cups dried medium or large shell pasta

For the sauce

1⅓ cups raw cashews

2 tablespoons lemon juice

1 teaspoon honey

1 teaspoon white (*shiro*) miso

¼ cup nutritional yeast (optional)

¼ teaspoon salt

⅔ cup water, boiling or hot

To make the brussels sprouts

1. Preheat the oven to 400°F and line a baking sheet with parchment paper.

2. In a medium bowl, toss the brussels sprouts with the olive oil and salt.

3. Spread evenly onto the prepared baking sheet. Keep the bowl in which they were tossed.

4. Roast for 10 minutes and then flip. Roast for 10 more minutes until the brussels sprouts are lightly charred and crisp. Remove from the oven.

To make the pasta

While the brussels sprouts are roasting, bring a large pot of salted water to a boil. Add the pasta and cook according to package instructions. Drain the pasta and transfer to the bowl in which the brussels sprouts were tossed with oil.

To prepare the sauce

1. While the pasta is cooking, make the sauce by combining the cashews, lemon juice, honey, miso, nutritional yeast, if using, and salt in a blender.

2. Add the water and process until smooth. The sauce should be thick but pourable. Add more water, if needed.

3. To serve, add the sauce and half of the brussels sprouts to the pasta and toss. Arrange on 4 serving dishes and scatter the remaining brussels sprouts over top.

TIMING TIP: You can cook the brussels sprout halves in 10 minutes by pan frying. Instead of tossing the brussels sprouts in the oil, heat the oil over medium heat in a nonstick skillet and cook the sprouts for 5 minutes without stirring, then stir to turn the sprouts over and cook for 5 more minutes without stirring. Remove from the pan and season with the salt.

PER SERVING: Calories: 455; Total fat: 26g; Total carbs: 45g; Fiber: 7g; Sugar: 5g; Protein: 15g; Sodium: 516mg

Penne with a Spiced Eggplant and Mushroom Sauce

VEGAN, DAIRY-FREE, NUT-FREE, SOY-FREE
SERVES 4 • PREP TIME: 5 MINUTES • COOK TIME: 25 MINUTES

The pleasant chewy texture of whole-wheat pasta is a perfect complement to the thick, rich, and robust eggplant and mushroom sauce. Deceptively easy to make, with a multitude of textures and flavors, and dressed up further with some fresh parsley and grated Parmesan cheese for garnish, this is a dish that is sure to impress.

2 tablespoons extra-virgin olive oil

1 medium onion, chopped

1 tablespoon minced garlic

1 small eggplant, cut into ½-inch cubes

1 (8-ounce) package cremini mushrooms, chopped

1 teaspoon dried oregano

½ teaspoon ground cumin

¼ to ½ teaspoon dried red chili flakes

½ cup red wine vinegar

6 sun-dried tomatoes, chopped

1 (14-ounce) can diced tomatoes

1½ cups whole-wheat penne pasta

Salt

Freshly ground black pepper

1. Heat the olive oil in a large saucepan over medium-high heat. Stir in the onion and sauté for a few minutes.

2. Stir in the garlic, sauté for another minute, and then add the eggplant and mushrooms. Cook for 8 to 10 minutes, stirring often, until the mushrooms begin to release their liquid and are browned slightly.

3. Add the oregano, cumin, red chili flakes, and red wine vinegar to the pan and stir for another few minutes.

4. Stir in the sun-dried tomatoes and canned tomatoes. Reduce the heat to medium-low, cover, and simmer, stirring often, for 15 minutes, or until the sauce has thickened.

5. While the sauce is simmering, bring a large pot of salted water to a boil. Stir in the pasta and cook according to package instructions.

6. Reserve ½ to ⅔ cup of the pasta cooking water and drain the pasta.

7. Season the sauce with salt and pepper and stir in the cooked pasta. Pour in as much of the reserved pasta cooking liquid as needed to thin out the sauce. It should be fairly thick, so it evenly coats the pasta.

8. Serve hot.

SUBSTITUTION TIPS: For a chewier texture and slight nutty flavor, use brown rice penne. Durum wheat pasta may also be used in place of the whole-wheat penne. Substitute 2 tablespoons tomato paste for the sun-dried tomatoes.

PER SERVING: Calories: 255; Total fat: 8g; Total carbs: 39g; Fiber: 9g; Sugar: 10g; Protein: 8g; Sodium: 76mg

Panfried Baby Potatoes with Red Kale and Cabbage 101

Chapter 5

STIR-FRIES AND CURRIES

Stir-fries may be fast and easy to put together, yet they can shine on the dinner plate, too. Composed of more than just vegetables, these are straightforward meal solutions that often require only one pot or skillet and satisfy your nutritional requirements, all without much effort. The recipes in this chapter will also challenge and transform the common belief that because a stir-fry is fast, it's bland or boring. Also provided are some mouthwatering curries. Curry dishes available for takeout are often overly oily, sometimes bland, or maybe too spicy. As the cook, you get to control the amount of oil and heat that goes into your dishes. These recipes are fresh, vibrant, and wholesome, and they can be made in a hurry in your own kitchen.

Chipotle, Pinto, and Green Bean and Corn Succotash

VEGAN, GLUTEN-FREE, DAIRY-FREE, NUT-FREE, SOY-FREE
SERVES 2 • PREP TIME: 5 MINUTES • COOK TIME: 10 MINUTES

In just 15 minutes, you have a delicious, smoky, and zesty simple supper. It's about as quick and easy a dinner idea as you can get, and you can vary things up, too, by including other seasonal vegetables, even squash or grated root vegetables. Toss in a chopped jalapeño or two with the corn and green beans for extra heat.

2 tablespoons extra-virgin olive oil

1½ cups fresh or frozen corn

1 cup green beans, chopped

2 green onions, white and green parts, sliced

½ tablespoon minced garlic

1 medium tomato, chopped

1 teaspoon chili powder

½ teaspoon chipotle powder

½ teaspoon ground cumin

1 (14-ounce) can pinto beans, drained and rinsed

1 teaspoon sea salt, or to taste

1. Heat the olive oil in a large skillet over medium heat. Add the corn, green beans, green onions, and garlic and stir for 5 minutes.

2. Add the tomato, chili powder, chipotle powder, and cumin and stir for 3 minutes, until the tomato starts to soften.

3. In a bowl, mash some of the pinto beans with a fork. Add all of the beans to the skillet and stir for 2 minutes, until the beans are heated through.

4. Remove from the heat and stir in the salt. Serve hot or warm.

SUBSTITUTION TIP: If you don't have chipotle powder, smoked paprika is the best substitute, or use an additional ½ teaspoon chili powder and ¼ teaspoon cayenne pepper.

PER SERVING: Calories: 391; Total fat: 16g; Total carbs: 53g; Fiber: 15g; Sugar: 4g; Protein: 15g; Sodium: 253mg

Mixed Vegetable Medley

GLUTEN-FREE, NUT-FREE, SOY-FREE
SERVES 2 • PREP TIME: 5 MINUTES • COOK TIME: 20 MINUTES

There may be no better way to enjoy the fresh tastes of local summer produce than to stir-fry them in plenty of good-quality churned butter. Take advantage of what is local in your region and toss in any vegetables that are nearing the end of their shelf life. It's certainly a good way to get your daily dose of veggie goodness.

1 stick (½ cup) unsalted butter, divided

1 large potato, cut into ½-inch dice

1 onion, chopped

½ tablespoon minced garlic

1 cup green beans, chopped

2 ears fresh sweet corn, kernels removed

1 red bell pepper, seeded and cut into strips

2 cups sliced white mushrooms

Salt

Freshly ground black pepper

1. Heat half of the butter in a large nonstick skillet over medium-high heat. When the butter is frothy, add the potato and cook, stirring frequently, for 15 minutes, until golden. Turn the heat down slightly if the butter begins to burn.

2. Add the remaining butter, turn down the heat to medium, and add the onion, garlic, green beans, and corn. Cook, stirring frequently, for 5 minutes.

3. Add the red bell pepper and mushrooms. Stir for another 5 minutes, until the vegetables are tender and the mushrooms have browned but are still plump. Add more butter, if necessary.

4. Remove from heat and season with salt and pepper. Serve hot.

SERVING TIP: Serve over cooked rice and garnish with a dollop of sour cream.

SUBSTITUTION TIP: If fresh corn isn't available where you live, or you're making it out of season, 1½ cups of frozen corn can be used instead.

PER SERVING: Calories: 688; Total fat: 48g; Total carbs: 63g; Fiber: 11g; Sugar: 11g; Protein: 11g; Sodium: 360mg

Spicy Lentils with Spinach

VEGAN, GLUTEN-FREE, DAIRY-FREE, NUT-FREE, SOY-FREE
SERVES 4 ● PREP TIME: 5 MINUTES ● COOK TIME: 25 MINUTES

Silky and earthy iron-rich spinach is a satisfying and tempering accompaniment to spiced-up red lentils. Lentils are an excellent source of protein. Since very little prep time is required, most of the time is spent waiting for things to cook, so get a pot of rice simmering to serve with the cooked lentils for a balanced and complete meal.

1 cup dried red lentils, well-rinsed	½ teaspoon turmeric
2½ cups water	¼ teaspoon cayenne pepper
1 tablespoon extra-virgin olive oil	1 medium tomato, chopped
1 tablespoon minced garlic	1 (16-ounce) package spinach
1 teaspoon ground cumin	1 teaspoon salt
½ teaspoon ground coriander	Freshly ground black pepper

1. In a medium saucepan, bring the lentils and water to a boil.
2. Partially cover the pot, reduce the heat to medium, and simmer, stirring occasionally, until the lentils are tender, about 15 minutes.
3. Drain the lentils and set aside.
4. In a large nonstick skillet, heat the olive oil over medium heat. When hot, add the garlic, cumin, coriander, turmeric, and cayenne. Sauté for 2 minutes.
5. Stir in the tomato and cook for another 3 to 5 minutes, until the tomato begins to break apart and the mixture thickens somewhat.
6. Add handfuls of the spinach at a time, stirring until wilted.
7. Stir in the drained lentils and cook for another few minutes.
8. Season with salt and freshly ground black pepper and serve hot.

MAKE IT FASTER: Use 1 (14-ounce) can lentils, any unseasoned variety, instead of dried. Add them to the pan after the spinach has wilted.

PER SERVING: Calories: 237; Total fat: 5g; Total carbs: 35g; Fiber: 18g; Sugar: 2g; Protein: 16g; Sodium: 677mg

Pinto and Green Bean Fry with Couscous

VEGAN, DAIRY-FREE, NUT-FREE, SOY-FREE
SERVES 4 ● PREP TIME: 5 MINUTES ● COOK TIME: 15 MINUTES

This simple and zesty Mexican-style stir-fry is a colorful, well-balanced meal with the addition of pinto beans, crunchy green beans, and sweet corn. Couscous soaks up the tomato and spices and fills out the dish, but a cup of any cooked grain, such as rice or quinoa, will work just as well. Stir in some chopped jalapeños or chipotle powder for more heat.

½ cup water

⅓ cup couscous (semolina or whole-wheat)

2 tablespoons extra-virgin olive oil

1 small onion, chopped

½ tablespoon minced garlic

1 cup green beans, cut into 1-inch pieces

1 cup fresh or frozen corn

1½ teaspoons chili powder

½ teaspoon ground cumin

1 large tomato, finely chopped

1 (14-ounce) can pinto beans, drained and rinsed

1 teaspoon salt

1. Bring the water to a boil in a small saucepan. Remove from the heat and stir in the couscous. Cover the pan and let sit for 10 minutes.

2. Gently fluff the couscous with a fork.

3. While the couscous is cooking, heat the olive oil in a large skillet over medium heat. Add the onion and garlic and stir for 1 minute. Add the green beans and stir for 4 minutes, until they begin to soften. Add the corn, stir for another 2 minutes, then add the chili powder and cumin, and stir to coat the vegetables.

4. Add the tomato and simmer for 3 or 4 minutes. Stir in the pinto beans and couscous and cook for 3 to 4 minutes, until everything is heated throughout. Stir often.

5. Stir in the salt and serve hot or warm.

PER SERVING: Calories: 267; Total fat: 8g; Total carbs: 41g; Fiber: 10g; Sugar: 4g; Protein: 10g; Sodium: 601mg

Indonesian-Style Spicy Fried Tempeh Strips

VEGAN, GLUTEN-FREE, DAIRY-FREE, NUT-FREE
SERVES 4 • PREP TIME: 5 MINUTES • COOK TIME: 20 MINUTES

Tempeh is a traditional high-protein Indonesian food of soybeans turned into a firm cake through fermentation. The fermentation process makes tempeh much more digestible than most soybean products, and its sturdy form makes it a versatile and ready-to-cook ingredient to keep on hand in the freezer. These crispy, chewy tempeh wafers in a spicy tomato glaze are easy to make and irresistibly delicious. Add more chili flakes for extra spice.

1 cup sesame oil, or as needed

1 (12-ounce) package tempeh, cut into narrow 2-inch strips

2 medium onions, sliced

1½ tablespoons tomato paste

3 teaspoons tamari or soy sauce

1 teaspoon dried red chili flakes

½ teaspoon brown sugar

2 tablespoons lime juice

1. Heat the sesame oil in a large wok or saucepan over medium-high heat. Add more sesame oil as needed to raise the level to at least 1 inch.

2. As soon as the oil is hot but not smoking, add the tempeh slices and cook, stirring frequently, for 10 minutes, until a light golden color on all sides.

3. Add the onions and stir for another 10 minutes, until the tempeh and onions are brown and crispy. Remove with a slotted spoon and add to a large bowl lined with several sheets of paper towel.

4. While the tempeh and onions are cooking, whisk together the tomato paste, tamari or soy sauce, red chili flakes, brown sugar, and lime juice in a small bowl.

5. Remove the paper towel from the large bowl and pour the sauce over the tempeh strips. Mix well to coat.

SERVING TIP: Serve warm over cooked rice or rice noodles or with steamed bok choy.

PER SERVING: Calories: 317; Total fat: 23g; Total carbs: 15g; Fiber: 1g; Sugar: 4g; Protein: 17g; Sodium: 266mg

Fried Rice and Vegetables

GLUTEN-FREE, DAIRY-FREE, NUT-FREE
SERVES 4 • PREP TIME: 5 MINUTES • COOK TIME: 25 MINUTES

This recipe, packed with nutrients, is easy to add even more vegetables to. Add some sliced celery with the mushrooms.

¾ cup uncooked short- or long-grain white rice

1½ cups water

2 tablespoons sesame oil, divided

2 large eggs, lightly beaten

2 carrots, diced

4 ounces (1¼ cups) sliced white mushrooms

1 tablespoon minced garlic

6 green onions, white and green parts, sliced and divided

2 tablespoons tamari or soy sauce

½ cup frozen green peas, defrosted

1. Rinse the rice and add to a small saucepan. Add the water and bring to a boil. Reduce the heat to low, cover, and simmer for 15 minutes, until the water is absorbed. Fluff with a fork and set aside.

2. While the rice is cooking, heat ½ tablespoon of the sesame oil in a large saucepan or wok over medium heat. Add the eggs and cook without stirring for 5 minutes, until the egg is dry. Remove to a plate and cut into small strips. Set aside.

3. Return the saucepan or wok to the heat. Heat the remaining 2½ tablespoons of sesame oil. Add the carrots and stir for 2 minutes.

4. Add the mushrooms, garlic, and the white parts of the green onions. Stir for 3 more minutes.

5. Add the cooked rice and tamari or soy sauce. Cook, stirring frequently, for 10 minutes, until the rice is sticky.

6. Toss in the green parts of the green onions, peas, and egg and stir to mix. Remove from the heat and serve hot with extra tamari or soy sauce, if desired.

MAKE IT FASTER: Stir the eggs in with the carrots or omit altogether to make the dish vegan. (If omitting the eggs, reduce the amount of sesame oil to 1½ tablespoons.)

PER SERVING: Calories: 271; Total fat: 10g; Total carbs: 37g; Fiber: 3g; Sugar: 4g; Protein: 9g; Sodium: 567mg

Spanish-Style Saffron Rice with Black Beans

VEGAN, GLUTEN-FREE, DAIRY-FREE, NUT-FREE, SOY-FREE
SERVES 4 TO 6 • PREP TIME: 5 MINUTES • COOK TIME: 25 MINUTES

All of your nutritional requirements for a meal are satisfied in one skillet in this colorful and hearty dish. Earthy and robust black beans, tender vegetables, and white rice make a balanced medley of flavors and textures. Combined, they provide a perfect balance of proteins, so just serve hot from the pan and enjoy.

2 cups vegetable stock

¼ teaspoon saffron threads (optional)

1½ tablespoons extra-virgin olive oil

1 small red or yellow onion, halved and thinly sliced

1 tablespoon minced garlic

1 teaspoon turmeric

2 teaspoons paprika

1 cup long-grain white rice, well-rinsed

1 (14-ounce) can black beans, drained and rinsed

½ cup green beans, halved or quartered

1 small red bell pepper, chopped

1 teaspoon salt

1. In a small pot, heat the vegetable stock until boiling. Add the saffron, if using, and remove from the heat.

2. Meanwhile, heat the olive oil in a large nonstick skillet over medium heat. Add the onion, garlic, turmeric, paprika, and rice and stir to coat.

3. Pour in the stock, and mix in the black beans, green beans, and red bell pepper. Bring to a boil, reduce the heat to medium-low, cover, and simmer until the rice is tender and most of the liquid has been absorbed, about 20 minutes.

4. Stir in the salt and serve hot.

INGREDIENT TIP: Saffron is rather expensive, but only a little is needed. Slightly sweet yet faintly bitter, the subtle flavor of saffron is uniquely unmatched, but it's not essential to the dish and can be omitted.

PER SERVING: Calories: 332; Total fat: 5g; Total carbs: 63g; Fiber: 9g; Sugar: 2g; Protein: 11g; Sodium: 658mg

Simple Lemon Dal

VEGAN, GLUTEN-FREE, DAIRY-FREE, NUT-FREE, SOY-FREE
SERVES 4 • PREP TIME: 5 MINUTES • COOK TIME: 25 MINUTES

This refreshing lentil dish is one of the easiest ones I make and also one of the most elegant. Essentially, the lentils simmer away with minimal attention. That leaves you time to get a pot of rice simmering to serve up with the dal for a meal complete with balanced proteins.

For the lentils

1 cup dried red lentils, well-rinsed

2½ cups water

½ teaspoon turmeric

½ teaspoon ground cumin

2 tablespoons lemon juice

⅓ cup fresh parsley, chopped

1 teaspoon salt

For finishing

1 tablespoon extra-virgin olive oil

2 teaspoons minced garlic

½ teaspoon dried red chili flakes or ¼ teaspoon cayenne pepper

1. Add the lentils to a medium saucepan and pour in the water. Stir in the turmeric and cumin and bring to a boil.

2. Reduce the heat to medium-low, cover, and simmer, stirring occasionally, for 20 minutes, until the lentils are soft and the mixture has thickened.

3. Stir in the lemon juice, parsley, and salt, and remove the pan from the heat.

4. In a small saucepan, heat the oil over medium-high heat. When hot, add the garlic and red chili flakes or cayenne, and stir for 1 minute.

5. Quickly pour the oil into the cooked lentils, cover, and let sit for 5 minutes.

6. Stir the lentils and serve immediately.

PER SERVING: Calories: 207; Total fat: 4g; Total carbs: 30g; Fiber: 15g; Sugar: 1g; Protein: 13g; Sodium: 589mg

Gingered Black-Eyed Peas with Black Tea

VEGAN, GLUTEN-FREE, DAIRY-FREE, NUT-FREE, SOY-FREE
SERVES 4 • PREP TIME: 5 MINUTES • COOK TIME: 25 MINUTES

Very little preparation and cooking time is required for this dish, yet the earthy goodness of black-eyed peas is complemented by the addition of brewed black tea, which adds smoky depth, along with zesty ginger and fresh lime. It pairs especially well with rice for a balanced and easily digestible, fairly light meal.

2 tablespoons extra-virgin olive oil

1 tablespoon minced garlic

1½ tablespoons minced or grated peeled fresh ginger

1 or 2 fresh green chiles, seeded and finely chopped

1 teaspoon ground cumin

½ teaspoon turmeric

2 (14-ounce) cans black-eyed peas, drained and rinsed

¼ to ⅓ cup fresh cilantro, chopped

1½ teaspoons salt

2 cups brewed black tea (from 2 tablespoons tea leaves or 2 tea bags)

2 tablespoons lime or lemon juice

1. In a large saucepan, heat the olive oil over medium heat. Stir in the garlic, ginger, and fresh chiles and sauté for a few minutes.

2. Stir in the cumin, turmeric, black-eyed peas, cilantro, and salt. Add the brewed tea and bring to a boil. Lower the heat to medium and simmer, uncovered, until thickened, roughly 10 to 12 minutes.

3. Remove from the heat, stir in the lime or lemon juice, cover, and let sit for 5 minutes to allow the flavors to blend.

4. Serve hot.

PER SERVING: Calories: 245; Total fat: 8g; Total carbs: 34g; Fiber: 12g; Sugar: 1g; Protein: 12g; Sodium: 585mg

Creamy Polenta with Sautéed Mixed Mushrooms

GLUTEN-FREE, NUT-FREE, SOY-FREE
SERVES 4 • PREP TIME: 5 MINUTES • COOK TIME: 25 MINUTES

Delectably creamy, buttery polenta is topped with succulent panfried mushrooms cooked in a simple red wine and herb sauce for a meal that makes an impression. Nothing about this dish is fancy or complicated, but the basic ingredients work together magically to make a beautiful plate that easily outshines more fancy and time-consuming preparations.

For the polenta

4 cups water or vegetable stock

1 teaspoon salt

1 cup yellow cornmeal

For the mushrooms

1 tablespoon extra-virgin olive oil

1 large shallot or small onion, finely chopped

2 cloves garlic, minced

1 (16-ounce) package sliced mixed mushrooms

½ cup dry red wine

1 teaspoon dried rosemary

½ teaspoon dried thyme

¾ cup vegetable stock

1 teaspoon cornstarch

Salt

Freshly ground black pepper

2½ tablespoons unsalted butter

To make the polenta

1. In a medium saucepan, bring the water or vegetable stock and salt to a boil. Slowly pour in the cornmeal, whisking as you go to avoid lumps.

2. Reduce the heat to low, cover, and simmer for about 12 minutes, stirring every few minutes, until the water is absorbed and the polenta has thickened.

continued ➤

To make the mushrooms

1. While the polenta is cooking, heat the olive oil in a large nonstick skillet over medium heat. Add the shallot or onion and garlic and sauté for a few minutes to soften.

2. Increase the heat to medium-high and stir in the mushrooms. Cook for 5 minutes.

3. Pour in the red wine, add the rosemary and thyme, and simmer for another 5 minutes, until most of the liquid has evaporated.

4. Whisk together the vegetable stock and cornstarch and pour into the pan. Simmer for another few minutes to thicken. Season with salt and pepper.

5. Stir the butter into cooked polenta until melted. Spoon polenta into serving bowls and top with sautéed mushrooms and their sauce.

LEFTOVER TIP: Press leftover polenta into small discs and panfry in oil over medium-high heat until golden on both sides. Top with any remaining mushrooms or tomato sauce.

PER SERVING: Calories: 265; Total fat: 12g; Total carbs: 31g; Fiber: 4g; Sugar: 3g; Protein: 7g; Sodium: 678mg

Panfried Baby Potatoes with Red Kale and Cabbage

VEGAN, GLUTEN-FREE, DAIRY-FREE, NUT-FREE, SOY-FREE
SERVES 4 • PREP TIME: 5 MINUTES • COOK TIME: 25 MINUTES

Much more than a humble side, gently spiced panfried potatoes come together with earthy kale and naturally sweet cabbage in this filling one-skillet dish. Bursting with fresh and wholesome flavors, it's likely to be the showstopper of the meal.

3 tablespoons extra-virgin olive oil

1 medium onion, thinly sliced

1 pound baby potatoes, halved

2 tablespoons water, divided

1 teaspoon ground cumin

½ teaspoon ground coriander

½ teaspoon turmeric

1 cup green or red cabbage, shredded or cut into thin strips

1 cup green or red kale, stemmed and leaves cut into thin strips

½ teaspoon chili powder

1 teaspoon salt

1. In a large nonstick skillet, heat the olive oil over medium heat. When hot, add the onion and sauté for 5 minutes.

2. Stir in the potatoes and fry, stirring occasionally, for 10 minutes.

3. Sprinkle in 1 tablespoon of water, cumin, coriander, and turmeric, and cover the pan. Cook for another 5 minutes, or until the potatoes are fork tender, stirring occasionally.

4. Stir in the cabbage, kale, and remaining 1 tablespoon of water. Cook, stirring often, until the kale begins to wilt.

5. Add the chili powder to the pan, reduce the heat to medium-low, and cook for another 5 minutes, until the cabbage is tender.

6. Stir in the salt and serve immediately.

SERVING TIP: To balance out the dish and for additional protein, serve with Simple Lemon Dal (see page 97).

PER SERVING: Calories: 183; Total fat: 11g; Total carbs: 20g; Fiber: 4g; Sugar: 2g; Protein: 4g; Sodium: 609mg

Yellow Split Peas and Rice with Cauliflower and Green Peas

VEGAN, GLUTEN-FREE, DAIRY-FREE, NUT-FREE, SOY-FREE
SERVES 4 TO 6 • PREP TIME: 5 MINUTES • COOK TIME: 25 MINUTES

This easy one-pot dish is known as a *kitchari* in India, where rice, split peas or lentils, vegetables, and a few basic spices are combined for simple everyday meals that contain all of your basic nutritional needs.

¾ cup dried yellow split peas

4 cups boiling water

3 tablespoons extra-virgin olive oil

1 medium onion, finely chopped

½ tablespoon minced fresh ginger

2 cups cauliflower, cut into 1½-inch florets

1 large tomato, chopped

½ teaspoon ground cumin

½ teaspoon chili powder

¾ cup long-grain white rice

⅔ cup fresh or frozen green peas

3 tablespoons lemon juice

1 teaspoon salt

1. Rinse the split peas and place in a large bowl. Pour the boiling water over the split peas and set aside.

2. While the split peas are soaking, heat the olive oil in a large saucepan over medium heat. Add the onion and ginger and cook, stirring often, for 3 minutes.

3. Add the cauliflower and stir for 2 minutes. Add the tomato, cumin, and chili powder and cook for 5 minutes.

4. Pour in the split peas and water and add the rice and green peas. Bring to a boil, reduce the heat to low, and cover. Simmer for 20 minutes, until the water is absorbed.

5. Remove from the heat and stir in the lemon juice and salt. Serve hot or warm.

SUBSTITUTION TIP: Use 1 (15-ounce) can of lentils in place of the split peas. Do not soak them in boiling water, reduce the cooking water to 1½ cups, and add the canned lentils shortly before the rice has finished cooked.

PER SERVING: Calories: 401; Total fat: 12g; Total carbs: 62g; Fiber: 14g; Sugar: 8g; Protein: 15g; Sodium: 614mg

Indian-Style Potatoes and Cauliflower with Chickpeas

VEGAN, GLUTEN-FREE, DAIRY-FREE, NUT-FREE, SOY-FREE
SERVES 4 TO 6 ● PREP TIME: 5 MINUTES ● COOK TIME: 25 MINUTES

This dry vegetable curry is a variation of a classic North Indian dish. Potatoes and cauliflower are simmered in a fragrant spiced tomato sauce with a zesty lime finish. For a protein-boosting twist, I've added plump chickpeas to accompany the potatoes and cauliflower. This nourishing and fulfilling one-pot meal can be balanced out even further by serving it with some steaming hot white rice, which can be cooked while the vegetables are simmering.

3 tablespoons extra-virgin olive oil

2 tablespoons minced fresh ginger

1 teaspoon turmeric

1½ teaspoons ground coriander

1 teaspoon ground cumin

¼ teaspoon cayenne pepper

2 large potatoes, cut into ½-inch wedges

2 cups cauliflower, cut into 1-inch florets

3 medium tomatoes, finely chopped

1 (14-ounce) can chickpeas, drained and rinsed

¼ cup fresh parsley or cilantro, chopped

2 tablespoons lime juice

Salt

Freshly ground black pepper

1. In a large nonstick saucepan, heat the olive oil over medium heat. Add the ginger, sauté for 1 minute, and then stir in the turmeric, coriander, cumin, and cayenne and cook for another minute.

2. Add the potatoes and cauliflower to the pan, stir well to coat, and fry, stirring often, for 5 minutes.

3. Stir in the tomatoes. Bring to a gentle boil, reduce the heat, and then cover and simmer over medium-low heat for 10 to 12 minutes, stirring often, until the vegetables are fork tender.

continued ➤

4. Add the chickpeas and parsley and cook for another 5 minutes or until most of the liquid has evaporated and the vegetables are tender.

5. Stir in the lime juice, season with salt and freshly ground black pepper, and serve hot.

PER SERVING: Calories: 358; Total fat: 13g; Total carbs: 54g; Fiber: 12g; Sugar: 9g; Protein: 11g; Sodium: 77mg

Red Lentil and Cauliflower Tomato Pilaf

VEGAN, GLUTEN-FREE, DAIRY-FREE, NUT-FREE, SOY-FREE
SERVES 4 TO 6 • PREP TIME: 5 MINUTES • COOK TIME: 25 MINUTES

This Indian-style dish is referred to as a *pulao* in India. A pulao or pilaf is a rice dish that includes other additions, such as vegetables, spices, and, as in this case, lentils. It's a nourishing one-pot meal with complete protein.

½ tablespoon extra-virgin olive oil

1 small red or yellow onion, finely chopped

½ tablespoon minced garlic

½ to 1 tablespoon minced fresh ginger

2 fresh green chiles, seeded and minced, or ½ teaspoon dried red chili flakes

1½ teaspoons ground coriander

1 teaspoon ground cumin

½ teaspoon turmeric

2 medium tomatoes, chopped

2 cups cauliflower, cut into 1½-inch florets

½ cup red lentils, well-rinsed

½ cup long-grain white rice, well-rinsed

2 cups water

3 tablespoons lemon juice

1 teaspoon salt

1. Heat the olive oil in a large saucepan over medium heat. Add the onion and sauté for 5 minutes. Stir in the garlic, ginger, and chiles and sauté for 1 minute.

2. Add the coriander, cumin, and turmeric.
Stir in the tomatoes and simmer for another 5 minutes, stirring occasionally.

3. Stir in the cauliflower, lentils, and rice and stir for 1 minute.

4. Pour in the water and bring to a boil over medium-high heat.

5. Reduce the heat to medium-low, cover, and simmer for 12 minutes or until the liquid is absorbed and the lentils are tender.

6. Turn off the heat, and stir in the lemon juice and salt.

7. Toss with a fork and serve hot.

PER SERVING: Calories: 227; Total fat: 3g; Total carbs: 42g; Fiber: 11g; Sugar: 5g; Protein: 10g; Sodium: 607mg

Chickpea, Cauliflower, and Potato Coconut Curry

VEGAN, GLUTEN-FREE, DAIRY-FREE, NUT-FREE, SOY-FREE
SERVES 6 ● PREP TIME: 5 MINUTES ● COOK TIME: 25 MINUTES

Chickpeas, cauliflower, and potatoes are a delicious combination on any plate, but coconut milk and a few spices impart wonderful additions of flavor and fragrance to this simple, thick, and hearty curry. It doesn't hurt that you're getting a healthy helping of protein, vitamins, and minerals at the same time. Serve with hot, fresh-cooked white rice for a complete meal.

1 tablespoon extra-virgin olive oil

1 tablespoon minced fresh ginger

1 teaspoon ground cumin

½ teaspoon turmeric

¼ to ½ teaspoon cayenne pepper

2 cups cauliflower, cut into 1½-inch florets

1 medium potato, cut into ¾-inch dice

1 medium carrot, diced

1 large tomato, chopped

⅔ cup coconut milk

1 cup water

1 (19-ounce) can chickpeas, rinsed and drained

1 red bell pepper, chopped

1 teaspoon garam masala

Salt

1. In a large nonstick saucepan, heat the olive oil over medium heat. Add the ginger and sauté for a few minutes. Stir in the cumin, turmeric, and cayenne and stir for another minute.

2. Add the cauliflower, potato, and carrot and cook for another few minutes, adding a few teaspoons of water as necessary to prevent sticking.

3. Stir in the tomato and cook for another few minutes. Pour in the coconut milk and water and stir in the chickpeas. Bring to a gentle boil. Reduce the heat to medium-low, cover, and simmer for 10 minutes, stirring occasionally.

4. Add the red pepper, garam masala, and few tablespoons of water if the mixture seems too dry. Cover and continue to simmer for another 10 minutes, until the sauce has thickened.

5. Season with salt and serve hot.

SUBSTITUTION TIP: Garam masala is an aromatic Indian spice blend that can be found at most supermarkets. If you don't have it, instead add ½ teaspoon ground cumin, ¼ teaspoon ground cloves, ¼ teaspoon ground cinnamon, and ½ teaspoon ground black pepper.

PER SERVING: Calories: 230; Total fat: 10g; Total carbs: 27g; Fiber: 7g; Sugar: 7g; Protein: 8g; Sodium: 30mg

Thai-Inspired Sweet Potato and Kidney Bean Soup 120

Chapter 6

SOUPS, STEWS, AND CHILIS

Soups and stews are the ultimate comfort food. During the cold months, nothing is quite like a steaming bowl of soup or a spicy, hearty chili to warm the body. During the summer months, soups are also highly prized when something lighter is what the body craves. Essentially one-pot creations, they are easy to prepare and usually require little attention, other than the occasional stir. Soups are also great for playing around with spices and seasonings to develop your own style. In this chapter, you'll find recipes to suit your nutritional needs and satisfy your cravings. There are cherished classics here, in addition to some with a tasty twist. Load them up with what's in season, fill them out with protein-rich legumes, or keep them delightfully light and simple.

Quinoa Soup with Corn

VEGAN, GLUTEN-FREE, DAIRY-FREE, NUT-FREE, OIL-FREE, SOY-FREE
SERVES 4 • PREP TIME: 5 MINUTES • COOK TIME: 20 MINUTES

This is one of the easiest soups you can imagine. Once you have chopped a few vegetables, all you do is combine everything in a pot, which gently simmers away with only an occasional stir. What really makes this soup special, though, is the addition of nutty quinoa. A nutrient-packed grain, it has the highest and most complete protein profile of all grains, contains more calcium than milk, and is a good source of iron, phosphorus, and B vitamins.

3 cups water or vegetable stock

½ cup quinoa, well-rinsed

½ teaspoon turmeric

½ teaspoon ground cumin

½ teaspoon celery seed (optional)

1 small onion, chopped

½ tablespoon minced garlic

1 stalk celery, finely chopped

1 small carrot, finely chopped

1 cup fresh or frozen corn

2 tablespoons fresh parsley or cilantro, chopped

2 tablespoons lemon or lime juice

Salt

1. In a medium saucepan, whisk together the water or stock, quinoa, turmeric, cumin, celery seed, if using, onion, garlic, celery, and carrot and bring to a boil. Reduce the heat to medium and simmer for 10 minutes.

2. Stir in the corn and cook for another 3 to 5 minutes, until the vegetables are tender.

3. Add the parsley or cilantro and cook for 1 minute.

4. Remove from the heat, stir in the lemon or lime juice, and season with salt. Serve hot or warm.

PER SERVING: Calories: 130; Total fat: 2g; Total carbs: 25g; Fiber: 4g; Sugar: 3g; Protein: 5g; Sodium: 23mg

Caribbean Sweet Potato Soup

VEGAN, GLUTEN-FREE, DAIRY-FREE, NUT-FREE, SOY-FREE
SERVES 4 • PREP TIME: 10 MINUTES • COOK TIME: 15 MINUTES

Coconut milk intensifies the rich, buttery flavor of sweet potatoes and makes this very simple soup a smooth and creamy delight. Sweet potatoes are an excellent source of beta-carotene, vitamin C, and potassium, but it's the warming Caribbean taste that will have you coming back for seconds.

1½ pounds (3 large) sweet potatoes, peeled and cut into 1-inch cubes

4½ cups vegetable stock

1½ tablespoons extra-virgin olive oil

1 large onion, sliced

¾ cup coconut milk

1 teaspoon salt

1 teaspoon chili powder

½ teaspoon honey (optional)

½ teaspoon freshly ground black pepper

1½ tablespoons lime juice

1. Add the sweet potatoes and vegetable stock to a large saucepan. Bring to a boil, reduce the heat to medium-low, and cover. Simmer for 12 minutes until the sweet potatoes are tender.

2. While the sweet potatoes are cooking, heat the olive oil in a skillet over medium heat. Add the onion and cook, stirring occasionally, for 6 to 8 minutes. Remove from the heat and set aside.

3. When the sweet potatoes are cooked, remove from the heat and purée with an immersion blender or in a countertop blender until smooth.

4. Return the sweet potatoes to the heat and stir in the coconut milk, salt, chili powder, honey, if using, and pepper. Simmer for 2 minutes and then stir in the onions and lime juice. Note that with the addition of honey, this dish will no longer be vegan.

5. Serve hot.

PER SERVING: Calories: 259; Total fat: 15g; Total carbs: 32g; Fiber: 6g; Sugar: 11g; Protein: 4g; Sodium: 790mg

White Bean and Cream of Asparagus Soup

VEGAN, GLUTEN-FREE, DAIRY-FREE, NUT-FREE, SOY-FREE
SERVES 4 • PREP TIME: 5 MINUTES • COOK TIME: 15 MINUTES

Puréed white cannellini beans lend a little more boldness and depth of flavor than one would ordinarily find in a cream of asparagus soup, but they take nothing away from the simplicity and elegance of this summer classic. Best of all, the added protein means that this doesn't have to be just a starter soup but can be served as a delightful, light summer lunch by itself.

1 tablespoon extra-virgin olive oil

1 large onion, chopped

1 (14-ounce) can cannellini (white kidney) beans, drained and rinsed

1 pound asparagus, chopped

2 cups vegetable stock

2 tablespoons lemon juice

3 cups water

1 teaspoon salt

Freshly ground black pepper

1. Heat the olive oil in a large saucepan over medium heat. Add the onion and cook for 5 minutes.

2. Add the beans and asparagus, and pour in the vegetable stock and lemon juice. Add the water and bring to a boil, then reduce the heat to low and simmer for 5 minutes, until the asparagus is tender.

3. Remove from the heat. Using tongs, remove and set aside a handful of the asparagus tips.

4. Purée the soup with an immersion blender or in a blender until smooth. Stir in the salt and plenty of freshly ground black pepper.

5. Serve hot or warm, garnished with the asparagus tips.

SUBSTITUTION TIP: Canned navy beans or pinto beans may be used in place of cannellini beans.

PER SERVING: Calories: 175; Total fat: 4g; Total carbs: 28g; Fiber: 11g; Sugar: 6g; Protein: 9g; Sodium: 557mg

Cream of Tomato Soup

VEGAN, GLUTEN-FREE, DAIRY-FREE, SOY-FREE
SERVES 4 TO 6 • PREP TIME: 5 MINUTES • COOK TIME: 20 MINUTES

Once you've tried this creamy and flavorful soup, you'll think twice before reaching for a canned version. Gently spiced and lightly seasoned, the depth of flavor in this silky soup has a deep flavor that's enhanced with peppery fresh basil. Of particular note, the creaminess comes from coconut milk and cashews, which first are blended together into a paste. Cashews are protein-rich and filling, too, so while the soup is still light, it's more substantial than most creamed tomato soups I've ever eaten.

For the paste

1 cup raw cashews

⅔ cup coconut milk

For the soup

2 tablespoons extra-virgin olive oil

1 medium onion, chopped

1 tablespoon minced garlic

1 (28-ounce) can diced tomatoes

½ cup tomato paste

1 teaspoon turmeric

½ teaspoon ground cumin

½ teaspoon chili powder

1 teaspoon oregano

¼ cup fresh basil, chopped

Salt

To make the paste

In a medium-bowl, cover the cashews with boiling water and let sit for 5 minutes. Drain and transfer to a blender, along with the coconut milk. Process into a smooth paste, adding water as needed for a fairly thick paste. Set aside.

To make the soup

1. In a large saucepan, heat the olive oil over medium heat. Stir in the onion and sauté for 5 minutes. Add the garlic and sauté for another few minutes.

continued ➤

2. Add the tomatoes, tomato paste, turmeric, cumin, chili powder, oregano, and the cashew paste. Simmer over low heat, stirring occasionally, for 10 to 15 minutes. Add water as desired for a thinner soup.

3. The soup can then be puréed in a blender or with an immersion blender, or left chunky.

4. Stir in the basil and season with salt. Serve hot.

MAKE IT FASTER: Skip the cashew paste and use 1⅓ cups of coconut milk or heavy cream instead, and add an additional 2 tablespoons tomato paste. Note that with the heavy cream, the recipe will no longer be vegan or dairy-free.

PER SERVING: Calories: 409; Total fat: 31g; Total carbs: 29g; Fiber: 7g; Sugar: 12g; Protein: 10g; Sodium: 102mg

Tomato Soup with Pasta and Chickpeas

VEGAN, DAIRY-FREE, NUT-FREE, SOY-FREE
SERVES 4 TO 6 • PREP TIME: 5 MINUTES • COOK TIME: 20 MINUTES

A complete meal in itself, this is one of those soups that work for just about any season. It's a substantial winter warmer when served piping hot with some crusty bread that you can dunk into the bowl and enjoy between spoonfuls. Or garnish it with a splash of fresh lemon juice and let the soup cool a bit for a satisfying and refreshing summertime meal.

⅓ cup fusilli or other spiral pasta

1 tablespoon extra-virgin olive oil

1 medium red onion, chopped

1 small carrot, finely chopped

1 tablespoon minced garlic

1 jalapeño pepper, seeded and finely chopped

1 teaspoon ground cumin

1 (14-ounce) can diced tomatoes

1½ teaspoons dried Italian seasoning

1 (14-ounce) can chickpeas, drained and rinsed

½ cup fresh or frozen green peas

1 teaspoon salt

Freshly ground black pepper (optional)

1. In a medium saucepan, bring salted water to a boil. Stir in the pasta and cook according to package instructions.

2. While the pasta is cooking, heat the olive oil in large saucepan over medium heat. When hot, add the onion and carrot, and sauté for 5 minutes.

3. Stir in the garlic and jalapeño pepper, and cook for another minute.

4. Add the cumin, tomatoes, and Italian seasoning and ladle in 1¼ cups of the pasta cooking water. Simmer until the pasta is finished cooking, or about 5 minutes.

5. Drain the pasta, add to the saucepan, stir in the chickpeas, and simmer f or another 5 minutes, adding water as necessary for a thicker or thinner soup.

6. Add the green peas and simmer for another 5 minutes.

continued ➤

7. Stir in the salt, adjust for seasoning, add some freshly ground pepper, if desired, and serve hot or at room temperature.

INGREDIENT TIP: If you don't have dried Italian seasoning, use ½ teaspoon each dried rosemary, thyme, and basil.

PER SERVING: Calories: 221; Total fat: 6g; Total carbs: 35g; Fiber: 8g; Sugar: 9g; Protein: 9g; Sodium: 608mg

Indian Yellow Split Pea Soup

VEGAN, GLUTEN-FREE, DAIRY-FREE, NUT-FREE, OIL-FREE, SOY-FREE
SERVES 4 TO 6 • PREP TIME: 5 MINUTES • COOK TIME: 20 MINUTES

Split pea soups are a classic comfort food, and this very simple and elegant spiced split pea soup is a light, creamy, and delicious option for both cool and warm weather. Split peas are a good source of fiber, minerals, and several B vitamins. But even better, they are a complete protein, containing all nine essential amino acids. Spice up this soup even more by adding a half teaspoon of ground cumin or a pinch of cayenne pepper.

¾ cup dried yellow split peas, well-rinsed

1 (14-ounce) can diced or crushed tomatoes

1 carrot, sliced or chopped

1 tablespoon minced fresh ginger

1½ teaspoons chili powder

1 teaspoon ground turmeric

6 cups water

1 teaspoon salt

¼ cup fresh parsley, chopped

1. In a large saucepan, combine the yellow split peas, tomatoes, carrot, ginger, chili powder, and turmeric. Pour in the water.

2. Bring to a boil, reduce heat to medium, and cover the saucepan. Simmer for 20 minutes, stirring occasionally.

3. Remove from the heat. If you want a smooth soup, purée the soup with an immersion blender or in batches in a blender until smooth.

4. Stir in the salt and parsley and serve hot.

MAKE IT FASTER: Use 1 (14-ounce) can of lentils in place of the dried split peas and simmer with the other ingredients for 10 minutes.

PER SERVING: Calories: 182; Total fat: 1g; Total carbs: 34g; Fiber: 14g; Sugar: 9g; Protein: 12g; Sodium: 697mg

Hungarian-Style Mushroom Soup

NUT-FREE
SERVES 4 TO 6 ● PREP TIME: 5 MINUTES ● COOK TIME: 25 MINUTES

This fragrant and creamy, vibrantly flavored, colorful soup is a mushroom lover's delight. Garnish with some chopped fresh dill, a sprinkle of paprika, some dried red chili flakes, and fresh parsley for an especially appetizing presentation.

2 tablespoons unsalted butter

1 medium onion, chopped

1 (8-ounce) package mushrooms, coarsely chopped

1 tablespoon hot paprika

1½ teaspoons dried dill

1½ tablespoons tamari or soy sauce

2 cups water or vegetable stock

1 cup whole yogurt

2 tablespoons whole-wheat or all-purpose flour

3 tablespoons lemon juice

½ cup sour cream

¼ cup fresh parsley, chopped

Salt

Freshly ground black pepper

---

1. In a large saucepan, heat the butter over medium heat. Add the onion and sauté for 5 minutes.

2. Raise the heat slightly, add the mushrooms, and sauté for another 5 minutes, until the mushrooms just begin to release their juices.

3. Stir in the paprika, dill, tamari or soy sauce, and water or vegetable stock. Reduce the heat to medium-low and simmer, uncovered, for another 5 minutes.

4. While the soup is simmering, whisk together the yogurt and flour.

5. Stir the yogurt mixture into the soup, cover, and gently simmer over low heat for another 10 minutes.

6. Stir in the lemon juice and remove the pot from the heat. Stir in the sour cream and parsley and season with salt and freshly ground black pepper, as needed.

7. Serve hot or warm.

SUBSTITUTION TIP: Whole milk or coconut milk may be used in place of the yogurt.

PER SERVING: Calories: 200; Total fat: 14g; Total carbs: 13g; Fiber: 2g; Sugar: 6g; Protein: 7g; Sodium: 384mg

Bean and Peanut Soup

VEGAN, GLUTEN-FREE, DAIRY-FREE, SOY-FREE
SERVES 4 TO 6 • PREP TIME: 10 MINUTES • COOK TIME: 20 MINUTES

This is an easy-to-prepare and hearty soup that is delicious spiced mild or hot. The warming combination of protein-packed peanuts, peanut butter, and black-eyed peas is inspired by West African cooking. If you like your soup spicy, add more ground cumin, dried red chili flakes, or even a dash of cayenne pepper.

1½ tablespoons extra-virgin olive oil

1 medium onion, chopped

2 medium carrots, sliced

2 celery stalks, sliced

2 (14-ounce) cans black-eyed peas, drained and rinsed

¾ cup unsalted peanuts

½ teaspoon ground cumin

½ teaspoon dried red chili flakes

3 cups water

⅓ cup natural peanut butter

1 teaspoon salt

Freshly ground black pepper

1. Heat the olive oil in a large saucepan over medium heat. Add the onion, carrots, and celery and stir for 5 minutes.

2. Add the black-eyed peas, peanuts, cumin, and red chili flakes, and stir for 1 minute.

3. Pour in the water and stir in the peanut butter, until well combined.

4. Bring the soup to a simmer and cook for 10 minutes, stirring occasionally. Add more water if you want a thinner soup.

5. Remove from heat and stir in the salt and freshly ground black pepper. Serve hot.

SUBSTITUTION TIP: Navy beans, cannellini beans, or pinto beans may be used in place of black-eyed peas.

PER SERVING: Calories: 412; Total fat: 29g; Total carbs: 26g; Fiber: 8g; Sugar: 5g; Protein: 19g; Sodium: 638mg

Thai-Inspired Sweet Potato and Kidney Bean Soup

VEGAN, GLUTEN-FREE, DAIRY-FREE, NUT-FREE, OIL-FREE, SOY-FREE
SERVES 6 • PREP TIME: 5 MINUTES • COOK TIME: 25 MINUTES

Sweet potatoes not only add a delightful creaminess to this hearty soup, but they're also an especially good source of beta-carotene and vitamin C. They combine here with robust and earthy, protein-rich kidney beans for a soup that is especially comforting on cold days.

1 (13.5-ounce) can coconut milk

2 cups water

2 shallots or 1 medium onion, finely chopped

2 teaspoons minced garlic

1 tablespoon minced fresh ginger

2 tablespoons Thai red curry paste

1 large sweet potato, peeled and cut into 1-inch cubes

½ teaspoon paprika

2 (14-ounce) cans kidney beans, drained and rinsed

2 tablespoons lime juice

1 to 1½ teaspoons salt

¼ cup fresh cilantro, for garnish (optional)

1. In a large saucepan, bring the coconut milk, water, shallots or onion, garlic, ginger, and curry paste to a boil over medium-high heat. Simmer for 5 minutes to blend the flavors.

2. Add the sweet potato and simmer, uncovered, for another 10 minutes.

3. Stir in the paprika and the kidney beans and simmer for another 10 minutes, or until the sweet potato is fork tender. Add more water as necessary.

4. Mash a few of the sweet potato pieces with the back of a spoon to thicken the broth.

5. Stir in the lime juice and season with salt. Serve hot, garnished with cilantro, if using.

PER SERVING: Calories: 311; Total fat: 17g; Total carbs: 33g; Fiber: 10g; Sugar: 7g; Protein: 9g; Sodium: 678mg

Stovetop "Baked" Beans

VEGAN, GLUTEN-FREE, DAIRY-FREE, NUT-FREE, OIL-FREE, SOY-FREE
SERVES 4 TO 6 • PREP TIME: 5 MINUTES • COOK TIME: 25 MINUTES

Baked beans are a classic comfort food, especially during the winter months. Though easy to prepare, they usually take at least an hour in the oven before they are ready to eat, but not with this recipe! Deep flavored, with hints of sweetness and smokiness, this modern take on an old classic pairs well with a side of rice and a lightly dressed leafy green salad.

2 medium tomatoes, diced

1 medium onion, chopped

2 (14-ounce) cans pinto beans, drained and rinsed

4 sun-dried tomatoes, chopped

1 jalapeño pepper, or 1 small green bell pepper, seeded and chopped

1 tablespoon Dijon mustard

1 tablespoon molasses

1 tablespoon pure maple syrup

2 tablespoons apple cider vinegar

1 teaspoon paprika

1 teaspoon ground cumin

1 cup water

1 teaspoon salt

Freshly ground black pepper

1. In a large saucepan, combine the tomatoes, onion, pinto beans, sun-dried tomatoes, jalapeño or bell pepper, mustard, molasses, maple syrup, apple cider vinegar, paprika, cumin, and water.

2. Bring to a gentle boil, reduce the heat to medium-low, and cover and simmer, stirring occasionally, for 20 to 25 minutes, or until the mixture thickens.

3. Stir in the salt and adjust for seasoning.

4. Serve hot, garnished with freshly ground black pepper and some extra maple syrup, if desired.

PER SERVING: Calories: 250; Total fat: 1g; Total carbs: 49g; Fiber: 14g; Sugar: 10g; Protein: 13g; Sodium: 577mg

Red Kidney Bean Chili

VEGAN, GLUTEN-FREE, DAIRY-FREE, NUT-FREE, SOY-FREE
SERVES 6 • PREP TIME: 5 MINUTES • COOK TIME: 20 MINUTES

You might be surprised to find out that this easy, rich, and robust red kidney bean chili is based on a classic North Indian curry called *rajma*. It tastes so much like a spicy Southwestern-style chili that no one would guess unless you told them it was Indian-inspired.

---

2 tablespoons extra-virgin olive oil

1 medium onion, chopped

1 tablespoon minced fresh ginger

½ tablespoon minced garlic

1 or 2 jalapeño peppers, seeded and chopped

1 (28-ounce) can diced or crushed tomatoes

2 teaspoons ground cumin

2 teaspoons chili powder

½ teaspoon ground cinnamon

3 (14-ounce) cans red kidney beans, drained and rinsed

1 tablespoon lemon juice

1 cup water

2 teaspoons salt

---

1. Heat the olive oil in a large saucepan over medium heat. Add the onion, ginger, garlic, and jalapeño peppers, and stir for 5 minutes.

2. Add the tomatoes, cumin, chili powder, and cinnamon. Simmer, stirring occasionally, for 10 minutes, until the tomatoes begin to thicken into a sauce.

3. Stir in the kidney beans and lemon juice and pour in the water. Simmer for 5 minutes.

4. Remove from the heat and season with salt.

PER SERVING: Calories: 596; Total fat: 6g; Total carbs: 47g; Fiber: 16g; Sugar: 9g; Protein: 17g; Sodium: 844mg

Tex-Mex Chili

VEGAN, GLUTEN-FREE, DAIRY-FREE, NUT-FREE, SOY-FREE
SERVES 6 ● PREP TIME: 5 MINUTES ● COOK TIME: 25 MINUTES

Rather than the more familiar addition of ground beef, protein-rich kidney beans and earthy mushrooms are the base of the bowl, along with an assortment of vegetables. To round out the meal further, sprinkle each portion with some grated cheese and serve with crusty bread or garnish with some sliced avocado and cilantro.

2 tablespoons extra-virgin olive oil

1 medium onion, finely chopped

1 medium carrot, cut into ½-inch dice

2 teaspoons minced garlic

1 red or green bell pepper, chopped

1 (8-ounce) package white mushrooms, chopped

1 tablespoon chili powder

1 teaspoon ground cumin

1 teaspoon dried oregano

1 (28-ounce) can crushed or diced tomatoes

1 (28-ounce) can red kidney beans, drained and rinsed

1½ teaspoons salt

Grated cheese (optional)

1. In a large saucepan, heat the olive oil over medium heat. Add the onion, carrot, and garlic and sauté for 5 minutes.

2. Add the bell pepper and mushrooms and sauté for another few minutes.

3. Stir in the chili powder, cumin, and oregano and toss to coat the vegetables. Add the tomatoes and simmer for 5 minutes, stirring occasionally.

4. Stir in the beans, reduce the heat to medium-low, cover, and simmer, stirring occasionally, for 10 to 15 minutes, until the vegetables are tender and the chili is fairly thick. Add more water if the chili seems too thick.

5. Stir in the salt and top with cheese, if using, but note that the addition of cheese will mean this recipe is no longer vegan or dairy-free.

PER SERVING: Calories: 210; Total fat: 6g; Total carbs: 32g; Fiber: 10g; Sugar: 7g; Protein: 11g; Sodium: 420mg

Chana Masala

VEGAN, GLUTEN-FREE, DAIRY-FREE, NUT-FREE, SOY-FREE
SERVES 6 • PREP TIME: 5 MINUTES • COOK TIME: 25 MINUTES

Chana masala is a classic North Indian dish that is enjoyed around the world, and if you've ever been to an Indian restaurant, there's a good chance you've seen it on the menu. This version preserves the essential contrast of aromatic and spicy flavors and may be served like you would a stew or chili. Garnished with some chopped cilantro and a few splashes of lemon juice, it goes especially well alongside steaming hot rice, which can be cooked while the chickpeas are simmering.

2 tablespoons extra-virgin olive oil

1 medium onion, chopped

2 teaspoons minced garlic

½ tablespoon minced fresh ginger

1 teaspoon turmeric

1 teaspoon ground cumin

1½ teaspoons chili powder

1 (28-ounce) can crushed tomatoes

2 (14-ounce) cans chickpeas, drained and rinsed

1 teaspoon garam masala

2 tablespoons lemon juice

1 teaspoon salt

1. In a large saucepan, heat the olive oil over medium heat. Add the onion and sauté for 3 minutes to soften. Add the garlic, ginger, turmeric, cumin, and chili powder and cook for another 2 minutes, stirring constantly.

2. Add the tomatoes, bring to a gentle boil, and simmer over medium heat for another 10 minutes to thicken.

3. Stir in the chickpeas, and simmer for another 10 minutes.

4. Add the garam masala, lemon juice, and salt and stir well to combine. Serve hot.

INGREDIENT TIP: Garam masala is an aromatic spice blend that can be found at most supermarkets. To prepare your own variation, while the chickpeas are simmering, combine ½ teaspoon black pepper and ¼ teaspoon each ground cinnamon and cloves.

PER SERVING: Calories: 241; Total fat: 7g; Total carbs: 36g; Fiber: 11g; Sugar: 12g; Protein: 11g; Sodium: 455mg

Creamy Chickpea and Portobello Mushroom Curry

VEGAN, GLUTEN-FREE, DAIRY-FREE, SOY-FREE
SERVES 4 • PREP TIME: 5 MINUTES • COOK TIME: 20 MINUTES

The portobello mushroom is often called the "steak" of vegetarian cooking for its sturdy and meaty texture and strong flavor. These mushrooms are also low-calorie, fat-free, and high in copper, selenium, and B vitamins. Portobellos combine with chickpeas and peanut butter in this thick, rich, and creamy spiced curry that's warming and filling, while providing a good helping of protein and nourishment.

2 tablespoons extra-virgin olive oil

1 medium onion, chopped

1 (14-ounce) can diced or crushed tomatoes

2 teaspoons curry powder

3 large portobello mushrooms, sliced

2 (14-ounce) cans chickpeas, drained and rinsed

2½ tablespoons natural peanut butter

½ cup water

1 teaspoon salt

½ tablespoon lemon juice

1. Heat the olive oil in a large saucepan over medium heat. Add the onion and stir for 5 minutes.

2. Add the tomatoes and curry powder and cook for 5 minutes, stirring often.

3. Stir in the mushrooms and cook for another 5 minutes, stirring often.

4. Add the chickpeas and peanut butter and pour in the water. Bring to a simmer, then reduce the heat to medium-low and cover the saucepan. Cook for 5 minutes, stirring occasionally. Add more water if the curry is too dry.

5. Remove from the heat and stir in the salt and lemon juice. Cover the saucepan and let sit for 5 minutes to allow the flavors to blend. Serve hot.

PER SERVING: Calories: 381; Total fat: 14g; Total carbs: 49g; Fiber: 15g; Sugar: 13g; Protein: 19g; Sodium: 684mg

Kidney Bean and Pumpkin Chili

VEGAN, GLUTEN-FREE, DAIRY-FREE, NUT-FREE
SERVES 6 • PREP TIME: 5 MINUTES • COOK TIME: 25 MINUTES

Canned pumpkin purée adds both creaminess and a vitamin- and mineral-dense ingredient to this robust and protein-rich chili. I like to add roughly chopped red bell peppers to the pot along with the tomatoes. For a refreshing finishing touch, stir in 2 tablespoons of fresh lime juice and garnish the servings with sour cream, chopped fresh herbs, or thin slices of jalapeño. For a complete meal, serve with a cooked grain, such as rice or quinoa, which you can easily have simmering while you prepare the chili.

1 tablespoon extra-virgin olive oil	1½ to 2 tablespoons chili powder
1 medium onion, chopped	1 teaspoon ground cumin
1 medium carrot, chopped	2 large tomatoes, chopped
1 tablespoon minced garlic	1 (15-ounce) can pumpkin purée
1 cup white mushrooms, chopped	1 (28-ounce) can kidney beans, drained and rinsed
½ tablespoon tamari or soy sauce	2 cups water or vegetable broth

1. Heat the olive oil in a large saucepan over medium heat.

2. When the oil is hot, add the onion and carrot and sauté for 5 minutes to soften.

3. Stir in the garlic and mushrooms and cook for another 5 minutes, stirring often.

4. Now stir in the tamari or soy sauce, chili powder, and cumin and cook for another minute.

5. Add the tomatoes to the pan and stir in the pumpkin purée, kidney beans, and water or vegetable broth.

6. Bring to a boil over medium-high heat, reduce the heat to medium-low, and cover. Simmer for 15 minutes, stirring occasionally.

7. Taste and adjust seasonings and serve hot.

INGREDIENT TIP: Not all chili powder is the same in terms of heat, and some blends are hotter than others. Remember you can always add more if the chili doesn't seem hot enough, but if you add too much, there's really no turning back. If that happens, stir in some yogurt or non-dairy milk to lessen the bite.

PER SERVING: Calories: 189; Total fat: 3g; Total carbs: 33g; Fiber: 11g; Sugar: 6g; Protein: 10g; Sodium: 116mg

Mediterranean Pita Pizzas with Olives and Goat Cheese 131

Chapter 7

PIZZAS AND FLATBREADS

Pizza is sure to please just about any number of tastes, as basic pizza dough and flatbreads provide a blank canvas that can be adorned with just about anything you please. The possibilities are as endless as the imagination of the cook. And it's certainly high on the list as one of the most popular ways to serve food around the world. In this chapter, you'll find twists on classic combinations as well as pizzas and flatbreads that use different bases upon which to showcase toppings and adornments. For the recipes that call for pizza dough, you can cut down on the prep time by purchasing prepared pizza bases. These are usually cooked at 350°F for 10 to 12 minutes.

Jalapeño Popper Mini Pizzas

NUT-FREE, OIL-FREE, SOY-FREE
SERVES 2 TO 4 • PREP TIME: 10 MINUTES • COOK TIME: 5 MINUTES

English muffin pizzas are kid and grown-up favorites alike; so easy and fast to make, they're a great afternoon or nighttime snack food. You can add any of the toppings you usually like on a pizza, but these mini pizzas have all the zesty cream cheese goodness of a jalapeño popper with extra cheesy flavor.

4 English muffins, halved

4 ounces (½ package) cream cheese, at room temperature

1½ cups shredded Monterey Jack cheese, divided

2 jalapeño peppers, thinly sliced

1 shallot, thinly sliced

1. Preheat the broiler and move the oven rack to the top level.

2. Place the English muffin halves on a foil-lined baking sheet and toast under the broiler for 1 minute to crisp.

3. Spread the cream cheese evenly over the English muffins. Sprinkle half of the grated Monterey Jack cheese over top.

4. Arrange the slices of jalapeño peppers and shallot on the English muffins, and sprinkle the remaining grated cheese over top.

5. Place under the broiler for 5 minutes, until the cheese is melted and bubbling.

TECHNIQUE TIP: Poke a fork in the crease of three sides of an English muffin and pull apart with your hands instead of using a knife. To slice jalapeños into rounds, cut off the stem ends and work a paring knife into the pepper around the seeds and core to remove them before slicing.

SUBSTITUTION TIP: Mozzarella, Cheddar, or a blend of shredded cheeses can be used.

PER SERVING: Calories: 773; Total fat: 48g; Total carbs: 55g; Fiber: 6g; Sugar: 3g; Protein: 35g; Sodium: 1054mg

Mediterranean Pita Pizzas with Olives and Goat Cheese

NUT-FREE, SOY-FREE
SERVES 2 ● PREP TIME: 5 MINUTES ● COOK TIME: 10 MINUTES

Pita breads form the crust for these quick and easy mini pizzas that can be served as a colorful lunch or a snack, or even as dinner alongside a green salad. Use any kind of pita bread—white or whole-wheat, with or without pockets. For a chewier pizza crust, purchase Greek pizza breads, which are usually thick and more bread-like.

---

2 (7½-inch) pita breads

¾ cup prepared tomato sauce

½ red onion, sliced

½ cup pitted black or Kalamata olives, sliced

½ cup soft, unripened goat cheese, cut into round slices

2 tablespoons extra-virgin olive oil

½ teaspoon dried oregano

½ teaspoon dried red chili flakes

---

1. Preheat the oven to 400°F.

2. Warm the pita breads for a minute in the oven or in a microwave.

3. Arrange the pita breads on a baking sheet and spread half of the tomato sauce on each pita bread.

4. Divide the red onion, olives, and goat cheese rounds between each pita bread.

5. Drizzle half of the olive oil over each pita bread, and sprinkle with oregano and chili flakes.

6. Bake the pizzas for 6 to 8 minutes, until the edges have just started to brown and crisp.

7. Remove from the oven and transfer to a cutting board. Cut into wedges and serve.

PER SERVING: Calories: 419; Total fat: 24g; Total carbs: 40g; Fiber: 4g; Sugar: 3g; Protein: 11g; Sodium: 674mg

Goat Cheese and Olive Bruschetta

NUT-FREE, SOY-FREE
SERVES 4 • PREP TIME: 10 MINUTES

Bruschetta is one of my favorite patio foods when the weather is hot. So easy to make: There's no cooking involved at all, unless you count quickly toasting or grilling a few slices of good-quality crusty bread. Any variety of toppings can be used, but chopped tomatoes are as close to essential as you can get.

8 thick slices of Italian bread

8 teaspoons extra-virgin olive oil

2 to 4 cloves garlic, crushed

1 (4-ounce) package soft, unripened goat cheese

¾ cup pitted green or black olives, sliced

2 medium firm tomatoes, diced

2 tablespoons fresh parsley, chopped

1 tablespoon fresh basil, chopped

Salt

Freshly ground black pepper

1. Toast the bread under a broiler until golden.

2. In a small bowl, whisk together the olive oil and garlic.

3. Brush each bread slice with a teaspoon of the olive oil and garlic mixture.

4. Spread each slice with an equal portion of goat cheese (about 1 tablespoon for each slice).

5. Top with the olives and tomato. Finish off by sprinkling each slice with fresh chopped parsley and basil. Season with salt and black pepper to taste and serve.

SUBSTITUTION TIP: Use ricotta, mascarpone, or dry curd cottage cheese in place of soft, unripened goat cheese.

PER SERVING: Calories: 305; Total fat: 16g; Total carbs: 35g; Fiber: 3g; Sugar: 2g; Protein: 8g; Sodium: 639mg

Mexican-Style Cheese and Pinto Bean Pizza

NUT-FREE, SOY-FREE
SERVES 4 TO 6 • PREP TIME: 5 MINUTES • COOK TIME: 15 MINUTES

Mexican ingredients make for a delicious pizza, and this is a fun way to serve pizza with fresh toppings on the side for people to help themselves. It's easy and especially tasty, if you're like most of us and love extra cheese on top.

For the pizza

Nonstick cooking spray, for greasing the pan

2 tablespoons yellow cornmeal (optional)

1 (16-ounce) store-bought pizza dough (thawed, if frozen)

4 cups shredded Monterey Jack cheese, divided

1 (14-ounce) can pinto beans, drained and rinsed

2 jalapeño peppers, sliced into rounds (optional)

Suggested toppings

Salsa

Guacamole

Sour cream

Sliced black olives

Fresh chopped cilantro

1. Preheat the oven to 475°F. Lightly grease a 12- to 16-inch pizza pan or round baking pan. Scatter the cornmeal, if using, over the surface of the pan.

2. Roll out the dough on a floured surface to fit the pizza pan. Transfer the dough to the pizza pan and stretch out the edges to form a ½-inch rim.

3. Scatter half of the shredded cheese over the dough. Scatter the pinto beans and jalapeño rounds, if using, over the cheese and then top with the remaining cheese.

continued ➤

4. Bake for 10 to 15 minutes, until the crust is golden brown.

5. Remove from the oven, cut into slices, and serve with suggested fresh toppings on the side.

INGREDIENT TIP: Cornmeal adds a delightful "grainy" texture to the pizza.

PER SERVING: Calories: 752; Total fat: 39g; Total carbs: 65g; Fiber: 10g; Sugar: 1g; Protein: 41g; Sodium: 938mg

Mushroom, Ricotta, and Asiago Cheese Pizza

NUT-FREE, SOY-FREE
SERVES 4 TO 6 ● PREP TIME: 10 MINUTES ● COOK TIME: 20 MINUTES

If you like mushrooms and cheese, then this is the pizza for you. Italian cow's milk Asiago cheese tastes similar to Parmesan but has a nuttier and slightly milder flavor that goes wonderfully on pastas, salads, or in this case, pizza.

2 tablespoons extra-virgin olive oil

1 (8-ounce) package sliced white or cremini mushrooms

½ tablespoon minced garlic

Nonstick cooking spray, for greasing the pan

1 (16-ounce) store-bought pizza dough (thawed, if frozen)

1½ cups prepared tomato sauce

1 cup shredded Asiago cheese

½ cup ricotta cheese

2 teaspoons dried oregano

1. Heat the olive oil in a skillet over medium-high heat. Add the mushrooms and garlic. Cook for 5 minutes, stirring frequently.

2. While the mushrooms are cooking, preheat the oven to 475°F. Lightly grease a 12- to 16-inch pizza pan or round baking pan.

3. For the pizza, roll out the dough on a floured surface to fit the pizza pan. Transfer the dough to the pizza pan and stretch out the edges to form a ½-inch rim.

4. Spread the tomato sauce over the pizza. Scatter the mushrooms and Asiago cheese over top. Use a small spoon to scoop small dollops of ricotta cheese on top.

5. Sprinkle the oregano over the pizza and bake for 10 to 15 minutes, until the crust is golden brown and the cheese is melted.

PER SERVING: Calories: 465; Total fat: 22g; Total carbs: 54g; Fiber: 5g; Sugar: 2g; Protein: 20g; Sodium: 862mg

White Bean, Artichoke, and Mushroom Pizza

NUT-FREE, SOY-FREE
SERVES 4 TO 6 ● PREP TIME: 5 MINUTES ● COOK TIME: 20 MINUTES

This no-sauce pizza is one of my favorites. It is easy to put together and combines some of the best flavors of Mediterranean food with the incredible taste of melted smoked Gouda cheese.

1 (8-ounce) package sliced white mushrooms

1 tablespoon water

Nonstick cooking spray, for greasing the pan

1 (16-ounce) store-bought pizza dough (thawed, if frozen)

1½ cups smoked Gouda cheese, shredded

1 (6-ounce) jar marinated and quartered or halved artichoke hearts, drained

1 (14-ounce) can cannellini (white kidney) beans, drained and rinsed

1 medium-firm tomato, thinly sliced

1 teaspoon dried oregano

1. Add the mushrooms and water to a skillet. Cook over medium-high heat for 5 minutes, stirring frequently.

2. While the mushrooms are cooking, preheat the oven to 475°F. Lightly grease a 12- to 16-inch pizza pan or round baking pan.

3. For the pizza, roll out the dough on a floured surface to fit the pizza pan. Transfer the dough to the pizza pan and stretch out the edges to form a ½-inch rim.

4. Sprinkle the pizza evenly with the shredded cheese. Arrange the mushrooms, artichoke hearts, beans, and tomato slices over the pizza and scatter the oregano over top.

5. Bake for 10 to 15 minutes, until the crust is golden brown and the cheese is melted.

PER SERVING: Calories: 405; Total fat: 12g; Total carbs: 60g; Fiber: 8g; Sugar: 3g; Protein: 20g; Sodium: 758mg

Hummus Pizza

NUT-FREE, SOY-FREE

SERVES 4 TO 6 ● **PREP TIME: 10 MINUTES** ● **COOK TIME: 15 MINUTES**

Sometimes the pizza craving hits and there's nothing else to do but satisfy it. You can pick up the phone and have a pizza delivered to your door, but nothing compares to homemade pizza, especially when you let your imagination work on the dough. For example, thick, creamy hummus is a perfect accompaniment to crusty breads and crackers, so why not spread a pizza crust with hummus instead of sauce and then top it off with cheese, onion, hot peppers, and olives?

Nonstick cooking spray, for greasing the pan

1 (16-ounce) store-bought pizza dough (thawed, if frozen)

1 cup shredded mozzarella cheese, divided

1½ cups prepared hummus (see page 149)

1 small red onion, sliced

2 jalapeño peppers, sliced

¼ cup pitted black or Kalamata olives, sliced (optional)

¼ cup grated Parmesan cheese

1. Preheat the oven to 475°F. Lightly grease a 12- to 16-inch pizza pan or round baking pan.

2. Roll out the pizza dough on a floured surface to fit the pizza pan. Transfer the dough to the pizza pan and stretch out the edges to form a ½-inch rim.

3. Sprinkle the pizza evenly with half of the shredded mozzarella cheese. Spread with hummus and then scatter the remaining mozzarella over top, followed by the red onion, jalapeño peppers, olives, if using, and Parmesan cheese.

4. Bake for 10 to 15 minutes, until the crust is golden brown and the cheese is melted.

PER SERVING: Calories: 460; Total fat: 18g; Total carbs: 60g; Fiber: 8g; Sugar: 1g; Protein: 22g; Sodium: 941mg

Sun-Dried Tomato Pizza with Olives and Cashew Cheese

VEGAN, DAIRY-FREE, SOY-FREE
SERVES 4 TO 6 • PREP TIME: 10 MINUTES • COOK TIME: 15 MINUTES

If you're looking to switch things up and make a vegan pizza, this one is loaded with tangy tomatoes, robustly flavored Kalamata olives, and a dairy-free cashew "cheese" sauce. Ground cashews and nutritional yeast blended with water and salt are the best friends of vegans who might otherwise miss the experience of cheese. Nutritional yeast is what gives the sauce its cheesy flavor and makes it a great addition to pastas as well. It can be found easily in any natural food store or most supermarkets.

For the cashew cheese

¾ cup raw cashews

1¾ cups water

2 tablespoons nutritional yeast

1 teaspoon salt

For the pizza

Nonstick cooking spray, for greasing the pan

1 (16-ounce) store-bought pizza dough (thawed, if frozen)

3 tablespoons balsamic vinegar

1 cup prepared tomato sauce

1 cup marinated sun-dried tomatoes, drained

½ cup pitted black or Kalamata olives, sliced

To make the cashew cheese

Add the cashews, water, nutritional yeast, and salt to a blender and process until smooth. Add water as needed. It should have the consistency of a fairly thick sauce.

To make the pizza

1. Preheat the oven to 475°F. Lightly grease a 12- to 16-inch pizza pan or round baking pan.

2. Roll out the dough on a floured surface to fit the pizza pan. Transfer the dough to the pizza pan and stretch out the edges to form a ½-inch rim.

3. Stir the balsamic vinegar into the tomato sauce and spread over the pizza. Spread the cashew cheese over the tomato sauce.

4. Arrange the sun-dried tomatoes and olives over top and bake for 10 to 15 minutes, until the crust is golden brown.

> **SUBSTITUTION TIP:** If you don't have nutritional yeast and are not concerned with keeping the pizza vegan, you can substitute grated Parmesan cheese in the cashew cheese mixture.

PER SERVING: Calories: 494; Total fat: 20g; Total carbs: 69g; Fiber: 10g; Sugar: 3g; Protein: 18g; Sodium: 1405mg

Coconut Roti with Cilantro Chutney

VEGAN, DAIRY-FREE, NUT-FREE, SOY-FREE
SERVES 2 • PREP TIME: 10 MINUTES • COOK TIME: 10 MINUTES

Roti are soft and round unleavened flatbreads native to Indian cuisine. There are many variations, but they are cooked in a hot skillet and commonly served as a curry accompaniment. Here I've made a simple dough that only requires a brief kneading and resting period. Pair roti with a quick home-made chutney to be served on top or on the side for a light meal solution.

For the roti

1 cup all-purpose flour

²/₃ cup unsweetened desiccated coconut

1 green chile, seeded and finely chopped

½ teaspoon salt

½ tablespoon extra-virgin olive oil

⅓ cup warm water

Oil, for greasing the pan

For the chutney

1 bunch fresh cilantro, stemmed and coarsely chopped

1 green chile, seeded and chopped

½ to 1 teaspoon ground cumin

1 tablespoon sugar

2 tablespoons lime or lemon juice

½ teaspoon salt

To make the roti

1. In a large bowl, combine the flour, coconut, chile, and salt.

2. Using your hands, work the olive oil into the mixture until well distributed.

3. Gradually add the water and combine until the dough is soft and not too sticky, just moist enough to shape into a small ball.

4. Knead the dough in the bowl with your hands for 3 minutes, until smooth and pliable. Cover with a clean kitchen towel and let rest for 10 minutes while you prepare the chutney.

5. Divide the dough into 4 pieces and press each ball into rounds that are roughly ¼-inch thick and 4 inches round.

6. Brush a large nonstick skillet with a bit of oil and heat over medium-high heat.

7. When hot, cook the roti, two at a time, for 2 to 3 minutes per side, until lightly browned. Transfer each roti to the kitchen towel, cover to keep warm, and repeat for the remaining roti.

8. Serve them on plates, and spoon chutney over top or on the side.

To make the chutney

In a blender, combine the cilantro, chile, cumin, sugar, lime juice, and salt. Process until smooth, adding a few teaspoons of water, if necessary, to get it going.

LEFTOVER TIP: Double the recipe for more servings, as leftovers may be wrapped in foil and reheated the next day in a preheated 180°F oven. Serve with leftover chutney or with a curry or soup to fill out a meal.

PER SERVING: Calories: 529; Total fat: 26g; Total carbs: 66g; Fiber: 9g; Sugar: 7g; Protein: 9g; Sodium: 1167mg

Mushroom Polenta Pizza

GLUTEN-FREE, NUT-FREE, SOY-FREE
SERVES 4 • PREP TIME: 5 MINUTES • COOK TIME: 25 MINUTES

Oddly, the question of whether the best way to enjoy pizza is to eat it using your hands or with a knife and fork can be a matter of rather intense debate. Really, it's a matter of personal preference and ultimately depends on what sort of pizza you are eating. In this case, a fork is required, as the "crust" is a soft polenta base. The polenta does brown nicely under the broiler, and, topped with rich and earthy herbed mushrooms, it's sure to please.

For the mushrooms

2 tablespoons extra-virgin olive oil

4 cups sliced white or cremini mushrooms

2 teaspoons minced garlic

1 teaspoon dried oregano

Salt

Freshly ground black pepper

For the polenta

2¼ cups water or vegetable stock

⅔ cup cornmeal

⅓ cup freshly grated Parmesan cheese

3 tablespoons unsalted butter

1 teaspoon dried rosemary

4 ounces Fontina cheese, cut into ¼-inch slices

To make the mushrooms

1. Heat the olive oil in large nonstick skillet over medium-high heat. Add the mushrooms and cook, stirring often, for 6 minutes, until the mushroom soften and begin to brown.

2. Stir in the garlic and oregano and cook for another minute. Season with salt and pepper and remove from the heat.

To make the polenta

1. While the mushrooms are cooking, in a medium saucepan bring the water or stock to a boil. Slowly whisk in the cornmeal to prevent clumping. Reduce the heat to medium-low and cook, stirring constantly to prevent sticking, for 6 to 8 minutes, until the mixture is fairly dry but still somewhat watery.

2. Remove the pan from the heat, and stir in the Parmesan, butter, and rosemary. Season with salt.

To assemble the pizza

1. Preheat the broiler and line a baking sheet with parchment paper.

2. Spread the polenta over the prepared baking sheet and shape into a 10-inch oblong or round, about ¾-inch thick.

3. Top with the Fontina slices and place the pan under the broiler until the cheese begins to bubble and brown, about 3 to 5 minutes.

4. Remove from the oven and spread the mushrooms evenly over top. Return to the oven and broil for another 2 to 3 minutes.

5. Cut into wedges, gently transfer to serving plates, and serve.

SUBSTITUTION TIP: Fontina is a semisoft cheese with a fairly mild, slightly nutty flavor. Provolone or Gouda is a suitable substitute.

PER SERVING: Calories: 378; Total fat: 28g; Total carbs: 20g; Fiber: 2g; Sugar: 2g; Protein: 14g; Sodium: 438mg

Chickpea Pita Wraps with Lemon-Tahini Sauce 152

Chapter 8

HANDHELDS

Sandwiches, burgers, and wraps are served and eaten daily in homes and in restaurants all over the country. It's no wonder, given the ease and convenience of both making and eating them. And there's no reason to think that vegetarian sandwiches or burgers are bland or boring, either—they're far more than just a few leaves of lettuce and chopped vegetables between slices of bread. In this chapter, you'll find an assortment of simple but unique, nourishing, and delicious vegetarian handhelds—from sandwiches, burgers, and wraps to tacos, burritos, and quesadillas—that can serve as appetizers or light lunches to full meals by themselves, all the while giving you vital control over the quality of the ingredients you're using.

Toasted Ciabatta Sandwiches with Goat Cheese, Sun-Dried Tomatoes, and Pesto

NUT-FREE, SOY-FREE
SERVES 2 TO 4 • PREP TIME: 5 MINUTES • COOK TIME: 5 MINUTES

This is a wonderfully delicious sandwich that looks pretty on a plate and hardly takes longer to put together than a basic tomato and cheese sandwich. Bursting with fresh flavor from a fast and easy homemade pesto, zesty dressing, and rounds of creamy goat cheese, dinner is complete with crusty bread. Served over a bed of mixed greens and with a scattering of robust black olives, this sandwich is dressed to impress without the fuss.

For the pesto

¼ cup sun-dried tomatoes, chopped

½ cup fresh basil, chopped

¼ cup extra-virgin olive oil

For the dressing

¼ cup extra-virgin olive oil

2 tablespoons lemon juice

1 teaspoon white vinegar

1 teaspoon salt

For the sandwich

1 medium ciabatta loaf or baguette, halved lengthwise

2 cloves garlic, halved

1 (4-ounce) package soft, unripened goat cheese, sliced into thin rounds

5 cups mixed greens, divided and chopped

½ cup sliced black olives

To make the pesto

In a food processor or blender, process the sun-dried tomatoes, basil, and olive oil into a thick paste. Set aside.

To make the dressing

In a small bowl, whisk together the olive oil, lemon juice, white vinegar, and salt.

To make the sandwich

1. Preheat the broiler and line a baking sheet with parchment paper.

2. Place the bread, face-side up, on the baking sheet and lightly toast. Rub with the garlic cloves and top with goat cheese slices. Return to the oven and broil until the cheese begins to bubble and brown.

3. Spoon pesto onto the bread, and top with roughly ½ cup of the mixed greens. Put the halves together to make a sandwich.

4. Using a serrated knife, slice the sandwich into diagonal portions.

5. To serve, line each plate with remaining salad greens and top with sliced sandwich. Scatter some olives over top.

MAKE IT FASTER: Purchase preprepared pesto and use ½ to ⅔ cup in place of the fresh pesto mixed with chopped sun-dried tomatoes.

PER SERVING: Calories: 530; Total fat: 33g; Total carbs: 44g; Fiber: 3g; Sugar: 4g; Protein: 14g; Sodium: 904mg

Mushroom and Cheddar Cheese Toasts

NUT-FREE, SOY-FREE
SERVES 4 TO 6 • PREP TIME: 5 MINUTES • COOK TIME: 10 MINUTES

These delightful cheese toasts are fast and easy to make and very addictive. They're perfect as an appetizer, but take care that you don't spoil your dinner by eating too many—these toasts could be a light dinner all on their own. Try sprinkling chopped red bell pepper or dried red chili flakes on top for a little color!

1 (12-inch) ciabatta bread loaf, cut into 1-inch slices

Unsalted butter, at room temperature

1 (8-ounce) package sliced white or cremini mushrooms

2 jalapeño peppers, seeded and finely chopped

⅔ cup sharp aged Cheddar cheese, grated

Salt

Freshly ground black pepper

1. Preheat the oven to 350°F and line a baking sheet with parchment paper. Arrange the bread slices on the pan.

2. Spread butter on each slice. Arrange the mushrooms and jalapeño peppers over the bread and top each slice with a scattering of Cheddar cheese.

3. Sprinkle each slice with salt and black pepper.

4. Bake for 10 minutes, or until the cheese is melted and the bread is toasted golden brown. Serve immediately.

PER SERVING: Calories: 554; Total fat: 28g; Total carbs: 57g; Fiber: 3g; Sugar: 1g; Protein: 14g; Sodium: 903mg

Hummus and Vegetable Wraps

VEGAN, DAIRY-FREE, NUT-FREE, SOY-FREE
SERVES 4 • PREP TIME: 10 MINUTES

Many people think of hummus as a snack or appetizer, but for someone like me, it's a meal! Served in generous spoonfuls in pita breads and topped with vegetables, it's simple, nourishing, and tasty—perfect for quick lunches or dinners. You can always buy hummus at the supermarket, but it's fast and easy to make at home, where you can use whatever spices you like.

For the hummus

2 (14-ounce) cans chickpeas, drained and rinsed

2 tablespoons extra-virgin olive oil

⅓ cup tahini

½ tablespoon minced garlic

3 tablespoons lemon juice

1½ teaspoons salt

For the wraps

8 (7-inch) pita breads

8 lettuce leaves

2 medium-firm tomatoes, chopped

1 red bell pepper, seeded and chopped

2 baby cucumbers, sliced or chopped

To make the hummus

Add the chickpeas, olive oil, tahini, garlic, lemon juice, and salt to a food processor and process until smooth. Add a little water if the hummus is too dry.

To make the wraps

Place a lettuce leaf in each pita bread. Spoon the hummus over the lettuce and top with chopped tomatoes, red pepper, and cucumbers.

TECHNIQUE TIP: If you don't have a food processor, mash the chickpeas in a large bowl with a potato masher and then stir in the remaining hummus ingredients until well combined.

PER SERVING: Calories: 741; Total fat: 23g; Total carbs: 111g; Fiber: 15g; Sugar: 12g; Protein: 26g; Sodium: 965mg

Pinto Bean and Avocado Burritos

VEGAN, DAIRY-FREE, NUT-FREE, OIL-FREE, SOY-FREE
SERVES 4 TO 6 • PREP TIME: 10 MINUTES • COOK TIME: 5 MINUTES

These zesty and creamy pinto bean and avocado burritos are delicious any time of year, but wrapping up vibrant Mexican-spiced goodness in handheld burritos seems especially suited to warm summer days. Apart from a bit of chopping, this fresh-tasting filling comes together in very little time. Spicy, cooling, and packed full of flavor, this one comes highly recommended.

For the filling

2 (14-ounce) cans pinto beans, drained and rinsed

1 avocado, pitted, peeled, and chopped

¼ cup fresh cilantro, chopped

2 tablespoons lime juice

1 teaspoon salt

2 medium tomatoes, chopped

1 jalapeño pepper, seeded and chopped

1 teaspoon chili powder

1 teaspoon ground cumin

For the burritos

8 (10-inch) soft corn or flour tortillas

Sour cream, for serving (optional)

To make the filling

1. Preheat the oven to 300°F.

2. In a medium bowl, toss the pinto beans, avocado, cilantro, lime juice, and salt in a medium bowl.

3. Heat the tomatoes, jalapeño pepper, chili powder, and cumin in a medium saucepan over medium heat for 5 minutes, stirring frequently.

4. Add the contents of the saucepan to the beans and stir to combine.

To make the burritos

1. While the tomatoes are cooking, wrap the tortillas in foil and warm for 5 minutes in the oven.

2. Spoon a generous helping of the filling into the center of a tortilla.

3. Fold in two sides of the tortilla over the filling, pressing down gently with your fingers.

4. Fold in the other two sides of the tortilla to completely close in the fillings. Flip the burrito over, pressing down firmly so the folds stay in place.

5. Use foil to wrap the burrito tightly and keep warm in the oven while you repeat with the remaining tortillas and filling.

6. Serve warm with sour cream on the side, if desired. Note that doing so will mean this recipe is no longer vegan or dairy-free.

PER SERVING: Calories: 378; Total fat: 9g; Total carbs: 63g; Fiber: 19g; Sugar: 3g; Protein: 16g; Sodium: 619mg

Chickpea Pita Wraps with Lemon-Tahini Sauce

NUT-FREE, OIL-FREE, SOY-FREE
SERVES 4 • PREP TIME: 10 MINUTES

The simple lemon tahini sauce in this recipe is so creamy, tangy, and heavenly, you'll find all kinds of uses for it. Chopped tomatoes and crunchy, tart pickles add texture and flavor to these wraps. If you have the time, you can make falafels yourself (see page 56) and use them in the pitas in place of the chickpeas for a truly authentic meal.

For the sauce

1¼ cups plain yogurt

¼ cup tahini

3 tablespoons lemon juice

½ teaspoon minced garlic

½ teaspoon salt

Freshly ground black pepper

For the wraps

1 (14-ounce) can chickpeas, drained and rinsed

1 teaspoon ground cumin

8 (7-inch) pita breads

2 medium-firm tomatoes, chopped

½ cup chopped dill pickles

¼ cup fresh parsley, chopped

To make the sauce

Whisk together the yogurt, tahini, lemon juice, garlic, salt, and pepper in a medium bowl. Cover and chill until ready to serve.

To make the wraps

1. Place the chickpeas in a mixing bowl and mash with a fork or potato masher.

2. Stir the sauce and the ground cumin into the chickpeas.

3. Spoon the chickpeas and sauce into the pita wraps and top with tomatoes, dill pickles, and parsley.

PER SERVING: Calories: 583; Total fat: 14g; Total carbs: 94g; Fiber: 10g; Sugar: 10g; Protein: 22g; Sodium: 932mg

Open-Faced Sandwiches with Creamy Coconut Mushrooms and Sun-Dried Tomatoes

VEGAN, DAIRY-FREE, NUT-FREE, SOY-FREE
SERVES 4 • PREP TIME: 5 MINUTES • COOK TIME: 10 MINUTES

Sandwiches are always a good alternative when you want a quick lunch or a light meal, and they don't have to be boring, either. In just under 20 minutes, you can sit down to a sandwich that really deserves the title "gourmet," even though it is so easy and fast to prepare. An especially good choice on a hot summer day when you don't want to labor over the stovetop, these are both satisfying and gluten-free, too, if you use your favorite gluten-free bread for the toast. Mushrooms are more than just a delicious and versatile ingredient; they're also good sources of fiber, protein, B vitamins, and a number of essential minerals.

1 tablespoon coconut oil or extra-virgin olive oil

1 (16-ounce) package white mushrooms, sliced

½ tablespoon minced garlic

½ cup coconut milk

¼ cup sun-dried tomatoes, finely chopped

1 teaspoon paprika

½ teaspoon dried oregano

½ teaspoon dried thyme

½ teaspoon sea salt

Freshly ground black pepper

4 thick slices crusty bread

2 tablespoons fresh parsley, finely chopped

1. Heat the coconut oil in a nonstick skillet over medium-high heat.

2. When the oil is hot, add the mushrooms and garlic to the pan and cook for 5 minutes, stirring occasionally, until the mushrooms begin to brown and give up their juices.

continued ➤

3. Reduce the heat to medium and stir in the coconut milk, sun-dried tomatoes, paprika oregano, thyme, salt, and pepper. Simmer for 5 minutes longer, until the sauce has thickened.

4. Toast the bread until nicely browned and transfer to serving plates.

5. Spoon the mushroom mixture over the bread slices and garnish with fresh parsley.

6. Serve immediately.

SERVING TIP: Serve the sandwiches over a bed of lightly dressed mixed greens and scatter some chopped black olives over top to really fancy them up. Unlike traditional sandwiches, this one is meant to be enjoyed with a knife and fork.

PER SERVING: Calories: 217; Total fat: 12g; Total carbs: 23g; Fiber: 3g; Sugar: 5g; Protein: 8g; Sodium: 493mg

Refried Bean Tacos

VEGAN, DAIRY-FREE, NUT-FREE, SOY-FREE
SERVES 4 ● PREP TIME: 5 MINUTES ● COOK TIME: 15 MINUTES

Refried beans are the ideal vegetarian replacement for seasoned ground beef in tacos, and not just because they're a good source of protein. They're a great vehicle for spices, can be just as easily spooned into taco shells or tortillas, and taste delicious with the same kinds of toppings you'd use for a beef taco. While you can always buy a couple of cans of prepared refried beans, making your own at home is easy and quick, and they taste much better, too.

For the refried beans

1 (14-ounce) can pinto beans, drained and rinsed

2 tablespoons extra-virgin olive oil

1 medium onion, finely chopped

1 medium tomato, finely chopped

2 jalapeño peppers, seeded and chopped

1½ teaspoons chili powder

1 teaspoon ground cumin

1 teaspoon salt

¾ cup frozen corn (optional)

For the tacos

8 (6-inch) taco shells or soft corn or flour tortillas

To make the refried beans

1. In a mixing bowl, mash the pinto beans with a fork or potato masher.

2. Heat the olive oil in a large nonstick skillet over medium heat. Add the onion and stir for 3 minutes.

3. Add the tomato, jalapeño peppers, chili powder, cumin, and salt. Cook, stirring frequently, for 5 minutes.

4. Add the mashed pinto beans and corn, if using, and cook for 5 minutes, stirring occasionally to coat the beans.

continued ➤

To make the tacos

1. If using taco shells, crisp in the oven according to package instructions. If using soft corn or flour tortillas, wrap in foil and warm for 5 minutes in a 300°F oven.

2. Spoon the refried beans into the taco shells or tortillas. Serve immediately.

INGREDIENT TIP: Add toppings such as shredded lettuce, shredded Monterey Jack or Cheddar cheese, diced tomato, salsa, sour cream, and fresh chopped cilantro to embellish the tacos.

PER SERVING: Calories: 375; Total fat: 17g; Total carbs: 48g; Fiber: 9g; Sugar: 3g; Protein: 10g; Sodium: 839mg

Portobello Mushroom Burgers

VEGAN, DAIRY-FREE, NUT-FREE, SOY-FREE
SERVES 2 TO 4 • PREP TIME: 5 MINUTES • COOK TIME: 20 MINUTES

Hearty portobello mushrooms are an excellent, utterly delicious substitute for traditional beef patties and surprisingly filling, too. A bit of heat from the addition of spices, along with some fragrant herbs and toppings of your choice, result in an unforgettable burger experience. The mushrooms can also be grilled, making them a fine option for the barbecue during the summer months.

4 medium portobello mushrooms

¼ cup extra-virgin olive oil

2 tablespoons balsamic vinegar

1 tablespoon minced garlic

1 teaspoon smoked paprika

1 teaspoon dried oregano

½ teaspoon dried thyme

½ teaspoon freshly ground black pepper

4 burger buns, halved and lightly toasted

½ to 1 cup baby spinach

1 large tomato, thinly sliced

1 small red onion, thinly sliced

1. Preheat the oven to 400°F. Wipe the mushrooms clean with a damp cloth. Place stem-side up in a baking dish.

2. In a small bowl, whisk together the olive oil, balsamic vinegar, garlic, paprika, oregano, thyme, and black pepper. Drizzle over the mushrooms and coat thoroughly with a pastry brush.

3. Bake for 20 minutes, until tender, turning halfway through the cooking time.

4. To serve, arrange each of the mushrooms over halved buns, top with baby spinach leaves, sliced tomato, red onion, and top with another bun.

SERVING TIP: Instead of burger buns, serve on English muffins or stuff the mushrooms in halved pita breads along with a selection of fresh vegetables and favorite sauces.

PER SERVING: Calories: 365; Total fat: 16g; Total carbs: 47g; Fiber: 5g; Sugar: 4g; Protein: 11g; Sodium: 457mg

Black Bean and Beet Burgers

VEGAN, DAIRY-FREE, NUT-FREE, SOY-FREE
SERVES 4 • PREP TIME: 10 MINUTES • COOK TIME: 25 MINUTES

Hearty black beans and nutty quinoa are a perfect complement to robust and nourishing iron-rich beets, especially with the addition of a bit of underlying heat and smokiness from spices. Enjoy these burgers served between lightly toasted burger buns loaded up with your favorite toppings. They can be gluten-free, too, if you use gluten-free buns.

⅓ cup quinoa, well-rinsed

⅔ cup water

1 (14-ounce) can black beans, drained and rinsed

1 medium beet (roughly 1 cup), peeled and grated

1 small onion, finely chopped

1 teaspoon ground cumin

1 teaspoon chili powder

½ teaspoon smoked paprika

½ teaspoon dried oregano

1 teaspoon salt

½ teaspoon freshly ground black pepper

2 tablespoons extra-virgin olive oil

6 burger buns, halved and lightly toasted

1. In a small saucepan, bring the quinoa and water to a boil, reduce the heat to low, and cover for 12 minutes, or until the liquid is absorbed.

2. While the quinoa is cooking, in a medium bowl, mash the beans with a fork or potato masher.

3. Mix in the beet, onion, cooked quinoa, cumin, chili powder, paprika, oregano, salt, and pepper until well combined.

4. In a large nonstick skillet, heat the olive oil over medium heat. When hot, shape the black bean mixture into roughly 2-inch patties and transfer to the pan.

5. Cook for 5 minutes, gently flip, and cook for another 3 to 5 minutes. Transfer to a plate lined with paper towels to absorb any excess oil.

6. Serve on burger buns, topped with desired toppings, such as salsa, sliced onion, sliced tomato, and pickles.

PER SERVING: Calories: 539; Total fat: 13g; Total carbs: 88g; Fiber: 11g; Sugar: 5g; Protein: 19g; Sodium: 928mg

Portobello and Quinoa–Stuffed Sandwiches

VEGAN, GLUTEN-FREE, DAIRY-FREE, NUT-FREE
SERVES 2 TO 4 ● PREP TIME: 5 MINUTES ● COOK TIME: 25 MINUTES

Succulent and earthy portobellos serve as the bun in this unique take on the idea of a "burger." Broiling the mushrooms really brings out their meaty texture and provides the base for a flavorful and protein-rich quinoa filling. They may be put together like traditional burgers, or served as open-faced sandwiches, for an essentially fuss-free and certainly healthy, satisfying meal idea.

½ cup quinoa, well-rinsed

1 cup water

2 shallots or 1 small onion, finely chopped

¼ cup extra-virgin olive oil

3 tablespoons tamari or soy sauce

3 tablespoons balsamic or red wine vinegar

1 teaspoon Dijon mustard

4 large portobello mushrooms

⅓ cup sun-dried tomatoes, finely chopped

1 teaspoon chili powder

¼ teaspoon cayenne pepper

¼ cup fresh parsley, chopped

Freshly ground black pepper

1. In a small saucepan, bring the quinoa and water to a boil. Reduce the heat to low, cover, and simmer for 12 minutes, or until the liquid is absorbed.

2. While the quinoa is cooking, in a small bowl prepare the marinade. Whisk together the shallots or onion, olive oil, tamari, vinegar, and mustard.

3. Wipe the mushrooms clean with a damp cloth, remove the stems, and, using a spoon, gently scrape out some of the membrane of the mushrooms. Place the mushrooms in a shallow pan, pour the marinade over top, and let sit for 10 minutes, turning once so the mushrooms are well-coated.

4. Preheat the broiler. Transfer the mushrooms to a broiler pan and broil for 10 minutes, until they have softened and begin to release their juices.

5. Stir the sun-dried tomatoes, chili powder, cayenne, parsley, and black pepper into the cooked quinoa.

continued ➤

6. Transfer the mushrooms to serving plates, top with quinoa filling, and serve open-faced or topped with another mushroom to make a sandwich.

PER SERVING: Calories: 455; Total fat: 28g; Total carbs: 39g; Fiber: 6g; Sugar: 2g; Protein: 16g; Sodium: 1280mg

Chickpea, Quinoa, and Vegetable Wraps

VEGAN, DAIRY-FREE, SOY-FREE
SERVES 4 TO 6 ● PREP TIME: 5 MINUTES ● COOK TIME: 25 MINUTES

In this perfectly balanced, protein-packed entrée, buttery chickpeas feature along with nutty quinoa and crunchy red pepper, all enveloped in a creamy and zesty cashew sauce. Once the filling is ready, simply wrap it up in soft tortillas and serve with favorite toppings, like chopped avocado, salsa, and chopped parsley.

½ cup quinoa, well-rinsed

1 cup water

1 cup raw cashews

2 teaspoons minced garlic

¾ cup almond milk or other non-dairy milk

2 tablespoons lemon juice

1 tablespoon extra-virgin olive oil

1 small onion, finely chopped

2 teaspoons chili powder

1 small tomato, finely chopped

1 red bell pepper, seeded and cut into thin strips

1 (14-ounce) can chickpeas, drained and rinsed

Salt

6 (10-inch) flour tortillas

1. In a small saucepan, bring the quinoa and water to a boil. Reduce the heat to low, cover, and simmer for 12 minutes, or until the liquid is absorbed. Remove from the heat and set aside.

2. In a food processor or blender, combine the cashews, garlic, almond milk, and lemon juice. Process until smooth.

3. Heat the olive oil in a large nonstick skillet over medium heat. Add the onion and sauté for 5 minutes. Stir in the chili powder, tomato, and red bell pepper and cook for another few minutes.

4. Stir in the chickpeas, cooked quinoa, and cashew paste and season with salt.

5. To serve, spoon the mixture over tortillas, fold over, and cut in half.

PER SERVING: Calories: 692; Total fat: 26g; Total carbs: 93g; Fiber: 11g; Sugar: 8g; Protein: 23g; Sodium: 826mg

Mushroom and Goat Cheese Quesadillas

NUT-FREE, SOY-FREE
SERVES 4 • PREP TIME: 5 MINUTES • COOK TIME: 25 MINUTES

Earthy browned mushrooms, creamy goat cheese, melted Fontina, and tart sun-dried tomatoes, all seasoned with some hot spices, make up the filling for these Mexican-inspired quesadillas. Quickly panfried until golden, these warmed tortillas may be served as a light entrée, an accompaniment to other dishes, or appetizer bites.

½ tablespoon extra-virgin olive oil, plus more for greasing the skillet

1 small red or yellow onion, finely chopped

1 teaspoon ground cumin

½ teaspoon smoked paprika

½ teaspoon chili powder

1 (8-ounce) package sliced white mushrooms

⅓ cup sun-dried tomatoes, finely chopped

1 or 2 jalapeño peppers, seeded and sliced into thin rounds

¼ cup fresh parsley or cilantro, trimmed and chopped

Salt

Freshly ground black pepper

1 (4-ounce) package soft, ripened goat cheese, crumbled and divided

½ cup Fontina or Provolone cheese, grated and divided

6 (7-inch) soft tortillas

1. Heat the olive oil in a large skillet over medium heat. Add the onion and sauté for 5 minutes. Stir in the cumin, paprika, and chili powder and sauté for another minute.

2. Increase the heat to medium-high, add the mushrooms, and cook for another 5 minutes, or until the mushrooms begin to brown and most of the liquid has evaporated.

3. Add the sun-dried tomatoes and jalapeño peppers and cook for another minute. Stir in the parsley or cilantro and season with salt and pepper. Remove from the heat. Stir in roughly ⅓ of each of the cheeses.

4. To assemble, sprinkle the remaining Fontina or Provolone cheese over 3 tortillas. Spread the mushroom mixture evenly on top of the tortillas, and dot with the remaining goat cheese. Top each one with the remaining tortillas and press down firmly.

5. Brush a nonstick skillet with olive oil and heat over medium heat. Transfer one of the quesadillas to the pan and cook for 2 minutes, gently flip with a wide spatula, and cook for another few minutes, until golden brown on each side. Repeat with the remaining quesadillas.

6. Slice the quesadillas into wedges and serve.

SERVING TIP: Top with sour cream, guacamole, and/or salsa.

PER SERVING: Calories: 394; Total fat: 17g; Total carbs: 44g; Fiber: 4g; Sugar: 7g; Protein: 18g; Sodium: 817mg

Raw Peanut-Butter-and-Chocolate Nut Squares 172

Chapter 9

DESSERTS

We all need a sweet treat from time to time, but that doesn't mean it has to be bad for you. In fact, the recipes in this chapter all focus on natural ingredients, emphasizing their sweetness and freshness, rather than excessive amounts of added sweeteners. Additionally, all of these desserts are quick to make. Whether you want to top off a dinner with something a little special or are looking for a healthy snack to keep you going throughout the day, you'll find ideas here to suit any number of occasions and needs.

Peach-Lime Lassi

GLUTEN-FREE, NUT-FREE, OIL-FREE, SOY-FREE
SERVES 2 • PREP TIME: 5 MINUTES

Fruit-and-yogurt beverages called lassis originated in India, where they know a thing or two about beating hot weather. Made from blended ice, yogurt, fruit, and frequently a little aromatic spice, lassis are simple to make, and they're delightfully cold, smooth, and creamy—satisfying like an ice cream milkshake but lighter and easier on the stomach, and with a refreshing tang. Lassis are a perfect vehicle for sweet, fresh peaches (which don't need to be peeled), and a small amount of ground cardamom gives a hint of spicy-sweet flavor and fragrance.

4 large or 6 medium ripe peaches, pitted and chopped

1½ cups ice cubes

3 cups plain yogurt

Juice and zest from 1 lime (or 3 tablespoons lime juice)

1½ tablespoons honey

¼ teaspoon ground cardamom (optional)

1. Place the peaches, ice cubes, yogurt, lime juice and zest, honey, and cardamom, if using, in a large blender and process until smooth and frothy.

2. Pour into tall chilled glasses and serve cold.

SERVING TIP: Top each glass with a sprig of fresh mint or a slice of fresh lime.

SUBSTITUTION TIP: Use 8 cups frozen chopped peaches instead of fresh peaches if you have a high-powered blender.

PER SERVING: Calories: 485; Total fat: 15g; Total carbs: 76g; Fiber: 7g; Sugar: 68g; Protein: 18g; Sodium: 204mg

No-Bake Almond and Cherry Energy Bites

VEGAN, GLUTEN-FREE, DAIRY-FREE, OIL-FREE, SOY-FREE
MAKES 14 (1-INCH) PIECES • PREP TIME: 5 MINUTES

Nuts are a vegetarian's go-to for a quick helping of protein, and when mixed with dried fruits and a little honey or maple syrup, they give you a good helping of raw energy. That's why I call these easy no-bake almond and dried cherry balls "energy bites," because that's just what they are. Mixed with a little cocoa, they satisfy the appetite as well as a sweet craving without any of the guilt. They also keep well in the refrigerator for at least a week, perfect for a dessert or midday snack.

1¼ cups almond meal

¼ cup sugar

3 tablespoons unsweetened cocoa powder

¼ cup honey or maple syrup

¼ cup almond butter

⅓ cup dried cherries

1. Add the almond meal, sugar, and cocoa powder to a medium bowl and mix.

2. Add the honey or maple syrup, almond butter, and dried cherries and stir until well combined. Note that if honey is used, the recipe will no longer be vegan.

3. Shape the mixture into 1-inch balls and serve.

TECHNIQUE TIP: To make almond meal from scratch, pulse 1 cup of almonds (raw, blanched, sliced, or slivered) in a food processor until reduced to a fine meal.

SUBSTITUTION TIP: Use peanut butter or dried cranberries in place of the almond butter or dried cherries.

PER SERVING: Calories: 115; Total fat: 7g; Total carbs: 13g; Fiber: 2g; Sugar: 9g; Protein: 3g; Sodium: 24mg

Raw Pistachio-and-Cashew Halvah

GLUTEN-FREE, DAIRY-FREE, OIL-FREE, SOY-FREE
MAKES 16 (1-INCH) PIECES • PREP TIME: 10 MINUTES

If you've ever had the opportunity to taste tahini halvah, chances are you won't forget it. Found everywhere in the Middle East, halvah is mainly composed of tahini, nuts, and honey, all pressed into a dense and irresistible cake. It's a guilt-free treat, too, high in protein, calcium, iron, and magnesium. Best of all, it's easy to make at home if you have a food processor, but be sure to use good-quality honey and tahini.

½ cup raw pistachios

¼ cup raw cashews

1 cup sesame seeds, divided

¼ cup tahini

¼ cup raw honey

1 teaspoon vanilla extract

1. In a blender or food processor, process the pistachios and cashews until coarse. Transfer to a medium bowl.

2. Stir in ¼ cup of the sesame seeds and the tahini, honey, and vanilla extract until well combined.

3. Sprinkle the remaining ¼ cup of sesame seeds onto a small plate or piece of waxed paper. Shape 1 tablespoon of the nut mixture into a small ball and roll in the sesame seeds.

4. Repeat with the remaining nut mixture. Chill in the freezer for 5 minutes before serving.

MAKE IT FASTER: ½ cup of almond butter, cashew butter, macadamia nut butter, pistachio butter, or hazelnut butter (but not peanut butter) can be used in place of the whole nuts. This will make a denser and less textured halvah.

LEFTOVER TIP: Store leftovers in the refrigerator in a sealed container for up to a month.

PER SERVING: Calories: 121; Total fat: 9g; Total carbs: 9g; Fiber: 2g; Sugar: 5g; Protein: 3g; Sodium: 6mg

Pumpkin Pie Pudding

VEGAN, GLUTEN-FREE, DAIRY-FREE, SOY-FREE
SERVES 4 ● PREP TIME: 10 MINUTES

Nothing could be simpler than whizzing up pumpkin purée with banana, avocado, pumpkin pie spices, and maple syrup into a smooth no-cook pudding that tastes like pumpkin pie filling. It's sweet without being too sweet, and rich and creamy.

2 medium just-ripe bananas, peeled

2 ripe avocados, pitted and peeled

¾ cup unsweetened pumpkin purée

⅓ cup natural peanut or almond butter

3 to 4 tablespoons maple syrup

1½ teaspoons pumpkin pie spice

1 teaspoon vanilla extract

Almond milk (optional)

Almond slivers (optional)

1. In a medium bowl, mash the bananas and avocados using a fork or potato masher.

2. Add the pumpkin purée, peanut or almond butter, maple syrup, pumpkin pie spice, and vanilla extract. Use an electric hand mixer or spoon to beat the ingredients together. If the pudding is too thick, stir in some almond milk to thin.

3. Place in the refrigerator to chill for 20 minutes or longer.

4. Serve in dessert glasses or small bowls, topped with slivered almonds, if desired.

MAKE IT FASTER: Use a food processor to combine all of the ingredients in steps 1 and 2 together.

SUBSTITUTION TIP: If you don't have pumpkin pie spice, use ½ teaspoon ground cinnamon with pinches of any or all of the following: ground ginger, ground nutmeg, ground cloves, or ground allspice.

PER SERVING: Calories: 412; Total fat: 26g; Total carbs: 43g; Fiber: 12g; Sugar: 23g; Protein: 8g; Sodium: 64mg

Quick and Easy
Peanut Butter Cookies

VEGAN, GLUTEN-FREE, DAIRY-FREE, OIL-FREE, SOY-FREE
MAKES 12 (1½-INCH) COOKIES • PREP TIME: 5 MINUTES • COOK TIME: 10 MINUTES

With just four ingredients and only eight minutes in the oven, the only patience you'll need to make these flourless and egg-free peanut butter cookies is waiting for them to cool down enough to eat. Soft, with a nice bit of crunch on the outside, they're not only the easiest baked cookies I make, but maybe my favorites, too. If you like peanut butter, you'll love the extra-rich peanutty flavor of these cookies.

1 cup natural peanut butter

¼ cup maple syrup

1 teaspoon vanilla extract

1 teaspoon salt

1. Preheat the oven to 350°F. Line a baking sheet with parchment paper.

2. In a large bowl, mix together the peanut butter, maple syrup, vanilla extract, and salt until well blended.

3. Scoop generous tablespoon portions of the dough onto the prepared sheet pan. With a fork, press the cookies down slightly and make crosswise indentations in the cookies.

4. Bake in the oven for 8 minutes, until the cookies begin to turn golden. Remove from the oven and let sit on the baking sheet for 10 minutes. Gently transfer the cookies to a wire rack and let cool completely.

LEFTOVER TIP: Store at room temperature in a covered container for softer cookies or in the refrigerator for firmer cookies.

PER SERVING: Calories: 156; Total fat: 11g; Total carbs: 10g; Fiber: 1g; Sugar: 7g; Protein: 7g; Sodium: 198mg

Chocolate Mug Cake

VEGAN, DAIRY-FREE, SOY-FREE
SERVES 2 • PREP TIME: 5 MINUTES • COOK TIME: 15 MINUTES

With just one bowl, a spoon, and two mugs, you'll have a freshly baked cake ready to eat, even before dinner is finished. This recipe makes enough for two generous servings, but if you want a little less, it can easily be shared by dividing each cake into smaller portions. Though this delectably moist, rich, and fudgy cake needs little additional adornment, you can dress it up further with a sprinkle or two of powdered sugar.

Oil or nonstick cooking spray, for greasing the mugs

6 tablespoons all-purpose flour

3 tablespoons sugar

2½ tablespoons unsweetened cocoa powder

½ teaspoon baking powder

¼ cup vegan dark chocolate chips

2 tablespoons vegetable oil

6 tablespoons almond milk

1 teaspoon vanilla extract

1. Preheat the oven to 350°F, and lightly grease two large oven-safe mugs with oil or cooking spray.

2. In a medium bowl, combine the flour, sugar, cocoa powder, baking powder, chocolate chips, vegetable oil, almond milk, and vanilla extract. Stir well to combine.

3. Pour the mixture evenly into the mugs, and bake in the oven for 15 minutes, until a cake tester or toothpick inserted into the middle comes out clean.

4. Transfer the mugs to a wire rack and let cool for 10 minutes. Turn out onto plates or enjoy right from the mug.

INGREDIENT TIP: Make sure to use vegan chocolate chips if you want to keep these vegan.

PER SERVING: Calories: 425; Total fat: 22g; Total carbs: 57g; Fiber: 3g; Sugar: 30g; Protein: 6g; Sodium: 63mg

Raw Peanut-Butter-and-Chocolate Nut Squares

VEGAN, GLUTEN-FREE, DAIRY-FREE, SOY-FREE
MAKES 16 SQUARES ● **PREP TIME: 10 MINUTES**

Peanuts and chocolate are an irresistible classic combination. This protein-packed treat comes together quickly with the help of a food processor and a wee bit of patience while the squares chill in the freezer. Naturally sweetened with a small amount of pure maple syrup or honey, featuring peanut butter and an assortment of nuts in all their raw glory, and topped with delectable dark chocolate, these bars are healthy enough to eat for breakfast and are an essentially guilt-free dessert. You may be tempted to eat more than one square, but they are so filling, satisfying, and wholesome that you'll be happy to have leftover bars to enjoy for a few days.

For the squares

½ cup walnut pieces

½ cup raw almonds

1 cup raw cashews

1 cup unsweetened desiccated coconut

⅔ cup natural peanut butter

⅓ cup coconut oil, melted

⅓ cup maple syrup

1 tablespoon vanilla extract

½ teaspoon sea salt

For the topping

½ cup vegan dark chocolate chips

1 teaspoon coconut oil

To make the squares

1. In a food processor, process the walnuts, almonds, and cashews until the mixture is reduced to coarse crumbs.

2. Add the coconut, peanut butter, coconut oil, maple syrup, vanilla extract, and sea salt and process until the mixture is well blended and begins to hold together.

3. Transfer the mixture to an 8-by-8-inch baking pan. Press the mixture down firmly using the back of a spoon or with a piece of wax paper or parchment paper.

4. Put the pan in the freezer while you prepare the topping.

To make the topping

1. Melt the chocolate chips and coconut oil in a small saucepan over medium-heat, stirring often to prevent the chocolate from burning.

2. Remove the pan from the freezer. Pour the melted chocolate on top and spread evenly.

3. Return the pan to the freezer for 10 minutes, until the chocolate is set.

4. Cut into 2-inch squares and serve.

LEFTOVER TIP: Store remaining bars in a well-sealed container in the refrigerator for up to one week.

PER SERVING: Calories: 272; Total fat: 23g; Total carbs: 12g; Fiber: 3g; Sugar: 6g; Protein: 6g; Sodium: 65mg

Fudgy Avocado-and-Pumpkin Brownies with Dried Fruit

GLUTEN-FREE, DAIRY-FREE, SOY-FREE
MAKES 12 1-INCH PIECES • PREP TIME: 5 MINUTES • COOK TIME: 20 MINUTES

While avocados are delicious on their own, their creamy texture lends them to salads, dressings, sauces, dips, and even desserts. These easy, fudgy brownies incorporate not only avocado, but also beta-carotene-loaded and potassium-rich pumpkin. They're vegan, too, if you use maple syrup and dairy-free dark chocolate chips.

1 ripe avocado, peeled and pitted

½ cup unsweetened pumpkin purée

½ cup natural peanut butter

2 tablespoons honey or maple syrup

¼ cup plus 3 tablespoons coconut milk

3 tablespoons unsweetened cocoa powder

1 teaspoon vanilla extract

¼ cup dried chopped fruit such as cherries or apricots

½ cup dark chocolate chips (regular or vegan)

1. Preheat the oven to 375°F. Line a standard 9-inch loaf pan with parchment paper and set aside.

2. In a blender or food processor, blend together the avocado, pumpkin purée, peanut butter, honey or maple syrup, coconut milk, cocoa powder, and vanilla extract until smooth. Stir in the dried fruit and chocolate chips.

3. Transfer the mixture to the prepared pan, spreading evenly.

4. Bake for 20 minutes, until a cake tester or toothpick comes out clean.

5. Let the pan cool on a metal rack for a few minutes and then cut into 1½-inch pieces. Refrigerate.

PER SERVING: Calories: 190; Total fat: 11g; Total carbs: 21g; Fiber: 4g; Sugar: 15g; Protein: 5g; Sodium: 10mg

Quick Reference Guide to Prepping and Cooking Vegetables

Veggie / Fruit	Prepping Options	Tools
ACORN SQUASH	Slice off stem, halve and remove seeds and pulp, then slice into wedges, purée, or dice	Chef's knife; spoon; food processor or blender
APPLE	Remove stem and core, slice, then purée, spiralize, halve, or dice	Paring knife; food processor or blender; chef's knife; spiralizer; mandoline
ASPARAGUS	Cut off bottom third of the stalk, at least, to remove more fibrous ends; peel into ribbons lengthwise, slice into thin disks, or purée	Chef's knife; vegetable peeler; food processor or blender
AVOCADO	Slice in half lengthwise, twist to separate, remove pit using a knife, slice into wedges or chunks, and slide a spoon between the flesh and skin to scoop out; purée or mash	Chef's knife; food processor; mortar and pestle
BASIL, MINT, SAGE	Roll or stack to thinly slice; mash using a mortar and pestle or purée	Chef's knife; food processor; mortar and pestle
BEETS	Slice off ends and peel, chop, or dice; spiralize red beets; purée, peel into ribbons, or grate	Chef's knife; paring knife; vegetable peeler; spiralizer; food processor or blender; box grater
BELL PEPPERS	Place a pepper on a workspace with the stem facing up and slice the side "lobes" and the bottom off, then discard the seeds, pith, and top (which should be all connected as one piece); slice into lengths, dice, or purée	Chef's knife; food processor or blender

Raw / Cooked	Cooking Methods	Serving Ideas
Cooked	Roast; sauté; steam; braise; slow cooker; pressure cooker	Stuffed roasted halves; roasted wedges; soup
Raw / cooked	Roast; sauté; simmer; braise; bake; slow cooker; pressure cooker	Raw snack or dessert; baked into chips; roasted or raw salads; relish; add to puréed soups; applesauce; apple butter; pickled; pie; cake; smoothie; bread; purée and add to a vinaigrette; slaws
Raw / cooked	Roast; steam; sauté; simmer; slow cooker; pressure cooker	Salad; add to pasta, legume, grain, and vegetable dishes; soup; pickled; risotto; anything with eggs, such as quiche
Raw / cooked	Grill; fry	Add to salads, sandwiches, and pasta; guacamole; place wedges on toast and top with olive oil, salt, and pepper; anything with cooked eggs, such as omelets; add to smoothie; use in a sauce or dressing
Raw / cooked	Sauté; roast; simmer	Pesto; add to salads, vegetables, grains, legumes, pasta, and eggs; add to dressings and sauces; add to pizza and breads, such as focaccia
Raw / cooked	Sauté; roast; simmer; steam; bake; slow cooker; pressure cooker	Chilled soup with sour cream and dill; pickled; add to salads, pasta, grain, and vegetable dishes; add purée to breads and chocolate cake batter; ravioli filling or pasta dough; add spiralized noodles to soups or use as pasta noodles; bake as chips; raw slaws; sauté with butter and maple syrup
Raw / cooked	Roast; sauté; simmer; bake; grill; stir-fry; slow cooker; pressure cooker	Roast and peel, slice in half, seed, and drizzle with olive oil, plus capers, garlic, salt, and pepper; purée as soup; add to tomato sauces; stuff whole with grains and vegetables; add to salads, sandwiches, grains, legumes, and pasta; raw with a dip; add to bread; add to a soffritto of onion, celery, and carrots; add to sauces such as aioli

Veggie / Fruit	Prepping Options	Tools
BOK CHOY	Slice off root end and use whole or chop	Chef's knife
BROCCOLI	Trim fibrous ends and snap off leaves, peel off the outer tough skin, and separate florets by slicing through the stems; slice the stems into batons, thinly slice into disks, chop, or dice	Chef's knife; food processor or blender
BRUSSELS SPROUTS	Trim bottoms and remove any wilted or yellowed leaves, thinly slice, halve, or grate	Chef's knife; food processor fitted with a grater; mandoline
BUTTERNUT SQUASH	Slice off ends, cut the squash in two just above the bulbous end, stand on end, and peel with a sharp knife or vegetable peeler; scoop out seeds with a spoon; slice into wedges, chop, dice, purée, or spiralize	Chef's knife; food processor; blender; spiralizer
CABBAGE	Slice into wedges, thinly slice, or grate	Chef's knife; box grater
CARROT	Trim top and peel; slice, dice, grate, or peel into ribbons	Chef's knife; paring knife; box grater; vegetable peeler
CAULIFLOWER	Trim bottom and remove leaves; slice into steaks; cut off florets at the stems; chop or dice stems; grate into rice, purée, or mash	Chef's knife; paring knife; box grater; food processor or blender

Raw / Cooked	Cooking Methods	Serving Ideas
Raw / cooked	Braise; grill; sauté; simmer; roast; stir-fry; steam	Warm or raw salad; raw slaws; soup; ramen; add to grain, vegetable, and legume dishes; raw with a dip for an appetizer; pickled; add to a green smoothie
Raw / cooked	Bake; blanch; braise; fry; grill; roast; sauté; simmer; steam; stir-fry; slow cooker; pressure cooker	Add to egg dishes, such as casseroles and quiche; roast with olive oil, smoked paprika, salt, and pepper, and finish with lemon juice; stir-fry with other vegetables in sesame oil, and finish with soy sauce; add to raw salads, Buddha bowls, grains, legumes, and vegetable casseroles; roast and toss with pasta, capers, preserved lemon, grated Parmesan cheese, and toasted bread-crumbs; soup; add roasted broccoli to pizza toppings
Raw / cooked	Roast; bake; steam; braise; fry; sauté; grill; pressure cooker; slow cooker	Slice thinly for a raw salad with green onions and dried cranberries; roast with apples; make a hash with potatoes, onion, and apple cider vinegar; toss with garlic, spices, and olive oil and throw on the grill; bake into a cheesy gratin
Cooked	Roast; sauté; steam; simmer; slow cooker; pressure cooker	Stuff with grains and/or vegetables; spiralize into pasta; add to salads, grains, legumes, and vegetables; soup; risotto
Raw / cooked	Roast; braise; sauté; steam; grill; bake; stir-fry; slow cooker	Roast wedges rubbed with olive oil, garlic paste, salt, and pepper; braise red cabbage with olive oil, cider vinegar, brown sugar, and apple chunks; slaw; cabbage rolls stuffed with rice and vegetables; pickle for kimchi; topping for tacos
Raw / cooked	Roast; braise; sauté; steam; grill; bake; stir-fry; slow cooker; pressure cooker; simmer; steam	Raw in a salad; soup; slaw; soufflé; bread; cake; add to vegetable, grain, and legume dishes; simmer in a pan with butter, honey, and orange juice until all the liquid is gone except a glaze
Raw / cooked	Bake; blanch; braise; fry; grill; roast; sauté; simmer; steam; stir-fry; pressure cooker; slow cooker	Purée into a sauce; grate into rice for tabbouleh or risotto; roast whole, smothered with a spicy sauce; substitute it for chicken in many dishes; soup; pickle for kimchi; swap out potatoes in mashed potatoes; use in a gratin; toss with pasta, lemon, capers, and breadcrumbs

Veggie / Fruit	Prepping Options	Tools
CELERY	Trim bottoms; slice into long strips or dice	Chef's knife
CORN	Remove kernels by standing a cob up in a bowl lined with a towel. Anchor it with one hand, and slide a knife down the cob to slice off the kernels	Chef's knife
CUCUMBER	Peel, halve, and scrape out juicy seeds; slice into thin or thick slices, peel into long ribbons, dice, grate, or pickle	Vegetable peeler; chef's knife; paring knife; spoon; box grater
DELICATA SQUASH	Slice off the ends, halve, and scrape out the seeds; slice into half-moons or purée	Chef's knife; spoon; food processor or blender
EGGPLANT	Slice off the ends, slice into ¾-inch slices, sprinkle evenly with salt, lay in a colander to drain for 30 minutes, then rinse to remove the salt and pat dry; slice, chop, dice, mash, or purée	Chef's knife; colander
GARLIC	Peel; chop the bulbs, thinly slice, mince, or smash and lightly salt to form a paste	Chef's knife
GINGER	Peel with a spoon and trim; slice, mince, or grate	Spoon; paring knife; fine grater or zester
GREEN BEANS	Trim; slice lengthwise or slice crosswise on the diagonal	Paring knife; chef's knife

Raw / Cooked	Cooking Methods	Serving Ideas
Raw / cooked	Roast; braise; sauté; bake; stir-fry; simmer	Use for making stock soffritto; make a celery gratin; braise in broth with tomatoes and onions, and top with shavings of Parmesan; add to salads for crunch
Raw / cooked	Sauté; roast; simmer; steam; grill	Chowder; stew; add to tacos with black beans, tomatoes, and avocado with a squeeze of lime; sauté with pickled onion, basil, and tomatoes and stuff into peppers with a little cheese; risotto; toss with zoodles, mint, and tomatoes; make Mexican corn
Raw / cooked	Sauté; bake; stir-fry	Use in salads, especially Greek and Middle Eastern salads; make tzatziki; swap out bread for cucumber disks; pickled; chilled soup; make a sandwich with cream cheese and dill; add slices to jugs of water; sauté with a little butter, salt, pepper, scallions, and mint
Cooked	Roast; bake; sauté; simmer; grill; braise; steam; slow cooker; pressure cooker; stir-fry	Soup; stuff scooped-out half with grains, dried fruits, and other vegetables; drizzle with oil and garlic, sprinkle with salt, pepper, and cayenne, and roast; add to warm salads or Buddha bowls; use as a pizza topping; toss with pasta; add to tacos; purée to add to chilis and stews; bake into a gratin
Cooked	Bake; roast; sauté; simmer; grill; stir-fry; braise; slow cooker; pressure cooker	Mash into a dip such as baba ghanoush; marinate and grill for a sandwich with tomatoes and smoked mozzarella; lightly bread and bake in a tomato sauce topped with Parmesan; roast and stuff with a grain and pomegrante seed salad; simmer with tomatoes, onion, garlic, and balsamic vinegar and purée for a soup
Raw / cooked	Roast; sauté; blanch; bake; stir-fry	Wrap a head of garlic with a drizzle of olive oil and a sprig of rosemary in foil and roast; sauté or roast chopped or thinly sliced garlic with vegetables, legumes, or grains; add to a soup with onions and thyme
Raw / cooked	Simmer; sauté; stir-fry	Tea; add to broths and soups; grate finely to add to fruit with a squeeze of fresh lime; add to miso and garlic paste to rub on vegetables; gingerbread; add to sauces or jams
Cooked	Blanch; sauté; simmer; bake; roast; stir-fry	Add to salads, soups, and grains; roast with olive oil, thyme, salt, pepper, and a squeeze of lemon

Veggie / Fruit	Prepping Options	Tools
JALAPEÑO PEPPERS, SERRANO CHILES	Trim off the stem, slice in half, and remove the seeds and pith; slice, dice, or mince	Paring knife
KALE	Fold leaves over the central tough rib, and remove the rib with a knife (not necessary for baby kale); coarsely chop	Chef's knife
LEEKS	Cut and discard the top part of the leek with tough, dark green leaves, split in half lengthwise, and feather under cold running water to remove dirt; slice into thin half-moons	Chef's knife
MANGO	Slice "cheeks" of mango off from stem to end, parallel and as close as possible to the long, flat pit; score the cheeks down to, but not through, the skin using the tip of a sharp knife; turn the cheek 90 degrees and score again. Scoop out the mango chunks using a spoon; purée	Paring knife; food processor or blender
MUSHROOMS, SMALL	Wipe clean with a paper towel and slice, quarter, or mince	Chef's knife
OLIVES (GREEN, NIÇOISE, KALAMATA)	Slice, smash using the flat side of a chef's knife, coarsely chop, or leave whole	Chef's knife
ONION, SHALLOT	Chop, dice, grate, or slice	Chef's knife
PARSLEY AND CILANTRO	Position a sharp knife at a 45-degree angle to the herbs and slice across the leaves to coarsely chop, including stems; gather the leaves and stems together and chop into smaller pieces or continue chopping to mince	Chef's knife

Raw / Cooked	Cooking Methods	Serving Ideas
Raw / cooked	Sauté; roast; bake; stir-fry	Roast with cornbread batter; roast with cheese; add to vegetable and legume dishes; pickle; add to cheese sandwiches or quesadillas; use in traditional tomato salsas or ones with diced pineapple and mango; jelly
Raw / cooked	Sauté; blanch; bake; roast; stir-fry; simmer; braise; grill; steam	Pesto; baked kale chips; sauté with lemon, olives, and capers, and toss with quinoa; add to soup; braise with garlic, dried chipotle chiles, and tomatoes; add to a green smoothie
Raw / cooked	Sauté; roast	Raw in salads; add to sautéed or roasted vegetables; roast halves in the oven with olive oil, salt, and pepper
Raw	Bake; grill	Smoothie; soup; sauces; relish with bell peppers, black beans, jalapeño, and shallots with a squeeze of lime juice; add to salads; add the purée to pound cake, muffins, pudding, ice cream, or sorbet; dry into fruit leather; spring rolls
Raw / cooked	Sauté; bake; stir-fry; roast; braise; grill	Coat with olive oil and a dusting of salt and pepper and roast at 400°F until well-browned; add to pasta and grain dishes; make mushroom risotto; stuff with peppers, garlic, breadcrumbs, and Parmesan cheese for an appetizer; use in casseroles
Raw / cooked	Sauté; roast	Add to pastas, grains, vegetables, and legumes
Raw / cooked	Bake; braise; fry; grill; roast; sauté; stir-fry; pressure cooker; slow cooker	Stuff sweet onions with grains and other vegetables and roast; caramelize and add to sandwiches, burgers, grains, and legumes; make a flatbread with caramelized onions, ricotta cheese, and herbs
Raw / cooked	Suitable for all kinds of cooking	Add to most vegetable, pasta, grain, and legume dishes, including roasts, soups, and casseroles

Veggie / Fruit	Prepping Options	Tools
PEACHES / NECTARINES	Peel and pit: for freestone peaches and nectarines, slice in half lengthwise, twist the halves apart, and remove pit; for non-freestone varieties, slice the peach from top to bottom, then slice a second time to create a narrow peach wedge, and pry it from the pit using the knife. Slice peach halves into wedges, dice, or purée	Chef's knife; food processor or blender
PEAS	Pry the shells open with your nails or a small knife, and remove the peas; purée or leave whole	Food processor or blender
PORTOBELLO MUSHROOMS	Wipe clean with a paper towel, and scrape out the gills using a spoon; leave whole or slice	Chef's knife; spoon
POTATOES, WHITE, RED, YUKON, FINGERLING	Peel (or not), slice, dice, mash, purée, grate, spiralize, or smash	Vegetable peeler; chef's knife; paring knife; potato ricer or masher; box grater; spiralizer; food processor (using pulse only); mandoline
RADISHES	Trim roots and tops; leave whole, halve, or thinly slice	Paring knife
SCALLIONS	Trim roots, and remove any outer damaged sheath; leave whole, slice in half lengthwise, or chop	Paring knife; chef's knife
SUGAR SNAP PEAS, SNOW PEAS	Trim ends and leave whole or thinly slice	Paring knife; chef's knife
SPAGHETTI SQUASH	Cut in half or leave whole; scoop out seeds and pulp with a spoon; after cooking, run the tines of a fork across the flesh to pull up "spaghetti" strands	Chef's knife; spoon; fork
SPINACH	Stack leaves, remove stems (not necessary for baby spinach), roll into a fat cigar shape, and thinly slice; gather slices together and mince	Chef's knife

Raw / Cooked	Cooking Methods	Serving Ideas
Raw / cooked	Bake; braise; grill; roast; sauté	Smoothies; soup; sauces; baste in butter, brown sugar, and cinnamon and grill; add raw peach slices to salads and grain dishes; make peach ice cream
Raw / cooked	Bake; blanch; braise; sauté; simmer; steam; stir-fry	Add to pasta, casseroles, soup, and vegetable dishes; purée for a pea soup; lightly sauté with salt and pepper, and toss with mint; add to an asparagus quiche or omelet
Raw / cooked	Grill; roast; sauté; braise; bake	Use in place of a bun for veggie burgers; stuff with vegetables, grains, or legumes; marinate in olive oil, balsamic vinegar, and garlic and roast or grill
Cooked	Bake; braise; fry; grill; pressure cooker; roast; sauté; simmer; slow cooker; steam; stir-fry	Twice-baked potatoes whipped with soft cheese topped with chives; spiralize and toss with olive oil, salt, and pepper, and roast until browned; grill slices of potato to add to salads; potato gratin; smash roasted baby red potatoes, sprinkle with salt, pepper, and dried rosemary, and drizzle with olive oil; roast; hash browns
Raw / cooked	Bake; braise; fry; stir-fry	Bake or roast with butter, salt, pepper, and parsley; add to salads
Raw / cooked	Braise; roast; grill; sauté; stir-fry	Toss in olive oil, salt, and pepper and roast or grill; pickle; add to salads, soups, pasta, grains, pizza, or legume dishes; add to any kind of egg dishes
Raw / cooked	Bake; braise; grill; roast; sauté; steam; stir-fry	Toss in olive oil, salt, and pepper and grill, then toss with chopped mint before serving; sauté and sprinkle with sea salt; sauté in sesame oil, and finish with lemon, salt, pepper, and sesame seeds
Cooked	Roast; bake; pressure cooker; slow cooker	Stuff with black beans, roasted red peppers, and onions, and top with cheese; toss strands with olive oil, Parmesan cheese, salt, pepper, and roasted pumpkin seeds
Raw / cooked	Blanch; braise; sauté; simmer; stir-fry	Sauté in a little olive oil, salt, and pepper, and toss with cooked quinoa, yellow raisins, and a squeeze of lemon; add to soups, salads, sandwiches, and pasta; mince for spanakopita

Veggie / Fruit	Prepping Options	Tools
STRAWBERRIES	Hull by cutting out the top stem; halve, thinly slice, dice, or purée	Paring knife; food processor or blender
SWEET POTATOES	Peel with a vegetable peeler; slice, dice, chop, grate, spiralize, or purée	Chef's knife; vegetable peeler; spiralizer; food processor or blender; box grater
SWISS CHARD, MUSTARD GREENS, DANDELION GREENS	Remove the central fibrous stem, if applicable, and stack several leaves on top of one another; fold in half lengthwise, roll into a fat cigar shape, and slice crosswise into wide or narrow ribbons; gather ribbons together and finely chop or mince	Chef's knife
TOMATOES	To peel a tomato, score the skin on the bottom of the tomato with an X, blanch in simmering water for 20 seconds, then dip in a bowl of ice water, and peel starting at the X; slice, chop, dice, grate, or purée	Paring knife or chef's knife; box grater; food processor or blender
ZUCCHINI, SUMMER SQUASH	Trim the ends and chop, dice, or slice into rounds, wedges, or matchstick lengths; grate using the largest holes of a box grater; spiralize	Paring knife or chef's knife; box grater; spiralizer; food processor or blender; mandoline

Raw / Cooked	Cooking Methods	Serving Ideas
Raw / cooked	Roast; sauté; grill	Roast and drizzle with balsamic vinegar for a sauce; purée for a sauce or to make ice cream; add to baked goods like cakes, scones, biscuits, and pies; pipe uncooked cheesecake batter into hulled strawberries; dice raw strawberries for salsas
Cooked	Roast; bake; sauté; simmer; grill; steam; slow cooker; pressure cooker	Baked and stuffed; spiralized; purée for a sauce, soup, or to add to pancake batter; add to stews and chili; enchiladas; tacos; season, roast, and add to warm salads and Buddha bowls; add to root vegetable roasts and gratins; baked sweet potato chips; sauté with butter and maple syrup; season and bake sweet potato fries; hash
Raw / cooked	Bake; blanch; braise; roast; sauté; simmer; steam	Use Swiss chard leaves for rolling up grains and vegetables, cover with a pasta sauce and cheese, and bake; sauté Swiss chard stems separately with garlic, salt, and pepper, finished with a vinegar drizzle; sauté garlic and onion, add broth, salt, and pepper, and braise mustard greens until tender; sauté dandelion greens in olive oil, garlic, salt, pepper, and red pepper flakes
Raw / cooked	Bake; blanch; braise; fry; grill; roast; sauté; simmer; stir-fry	Stuff raw with chickpea or lentil salad; slice in half and slow-roast with garlic, salt, and pepper; panzanella bread salad; tomato jam; salsa; Caprese; bruschetta; gazpacho
Raw / cooked	Bake; grill; roast; sauté; simmer; steam; stir-fry	Bake as fries: slice into wedges, toss in olive oil, salt, pepper, oregano, and Parmesan cheese; spiralize for spaghetti, then toss with tomatoes, basil, and garlic; slice in half lengthwise, then slightly hollow out to make boats and stuff with vegetables and grains topped with pasta sauce and cheese

The Dirty Dozen
and the Clean Fifteen™

A nonprofit environmental watchdog organization called Environmental Working Group (EWG) looks at data supplied by the US Department of Agriculture (USDA) and the Food and Drug Administration (FDA) about pesticide residues. Each year it compiles a list of the best and worst pesticide loads found in commercial crops. You can use these lists to decide which fruits and vegetables to buy organic to minimize your exposure to pesticides and which produce is considered safe enough to buy conventionally. This does not mean they are pesticide-free, though, so wash these fruits and vegetables thoroughly. The list is updated annually, and you can find it online at www.EWG.org/FoodNews.

Dirty Dozen™

1. Strawberries
2. Spinach
3. Kale
4. Nectarines
5. Apples
6. Grapes
7. Peaches
8. Cherries
9. Pears
10. Tomatoes
11. Celery
12. Potatoes

†Additionally, nearly three-quarters of hot pepper samples contained pesticide residues.

Clean Fifteen™

1. Avocados
2. Sweet corn
3. Pineapples
4. Sweet peas (frozen)
5. Onions
6. Papayas
7. Eggplants
8. Asparagus
9. Kiwis
10. Cabbages
11. Cauliflower
12. Cantaloupes
13. Broccoli
14. Mushrooms
15. Honeydew melons

Measurement Conversions

Volume Equivalents (Liquid)

US STANDARD	US STANDARD (OUNCES)	METRIC (APPROXIMATE)
2 tablespoons	1 fl. oz.	30 mL
¼ cup	2 fl. oz.	60 mL
½ cup	4 fl. oz.	120 mL
1 cup	8 fl. oz.	240 mL
1½ cups	12 fl. oz.	355 mL
2 cups or 1 pint	16 fl. oz.	475 mL
4 cups or 1 quart	32 fl. oz.	1 L
1 gallon	128 fl. oz.	4 L

Volume Equivalents (Dry)

US STANDARD	METRIC (APPROXIMATE)
⅛ teaspoon	0.5 mL
¼ teaspoon	1 mL
½ teaspoon	2 mL
¾ teaspoon	4 mL
1 teaspoon	5 mL
1 tablespoon	15 mL
¼ cup	59 mL
⅓ cup	79 mL
½ cup	118 mL
⅔ cup	156 mL
¾ cup	177 mL
1 cup	235 mL
2 cups or 1 pint	475 mL
3 cups	700 mL
4 cups or 1 quart	1 L

Oven Temperatures

FAHRENHEIT (F)	CELSIUS (C) (APPROXIMATE)
250°F	120°C
300°F	150°C
325°F	165°C
350°F	180°C
375°F	190°C
400°F	200°C
425°F	220°C
450°F	230°C

Weight Equivalents

US STANDARD	METRIC (APPROXIMATE)
½ ounce	15 g
1 ounce	30 g
2 ounces	60 g
4 ounces	115 g
8 ounces	225 g
12 ounces	340 g
16 ounces or 1 pound	455 g

Resources

There are countless videos on platforms like YouTube that feature cooking tutorials on everything from chopping an onion to preparing an entire meal. This is of particular value to novice cooks who find they learn best from visual examples.

Other websites for both veteran and novice cooks that I find invaluable include:

» **VegetarianTimes.com.** One of the largest collections of vegetarian recipes and lifestyle content online, *Vegetarian Times* has long been a magazine popular with established vegetarians and flexitarians alike. It's a useful resource with plenty of tried-and-tested recipes; an extensive glossary with definitions of ingredients and substitution suggestions; and a wealth of how-tos, from knife skills to recipe prep. Whether you are an established cook or just beginning to explore the joys of vegetarian cooking, you'll want to bookmark this site.

» **TheKitchn.com.** Updated daily, this site features articles about cooking instructions and recipes, in addition to product reviews and general kitchen advice. If you are looking for explanations and definitions about ingredients, substitutions, and methods, including planning and prep and tools you may encounter, then this site is sure to become a useful and interesting one that you should also bookmark.

» **Food52.com.** In addition to being an extensive source of inspiring and exciting, tried-and-tested, kitchen-approved recipes, you'll find plenty of instructional information and a shop, too, if you want to fancy things up a bit in your kitchen.

All of the sites listed above have highly searchable databases.

And do pay attention if you are visiting friends or relatives and food preparation is taking place. You'll be surprised how much you can learn from simply observing and asking questions—in my experience, cooks are always happy to share tips with others.

Index

191

Acknowledgments

Thanks to Barbara Isenberg of Callisto Media for her encouragement, editorial guidance, and assistance. A special thanks to my husband, David, for his support, patience, input, and editorial help.

About the Author

Lisa Turner is the cook and recipe developer behind Lisa's Cooking, found at FoodAndSpice.com, a blog that she founded in 2007 to share her passion for vegetarian food. She has been following a vegetarian diet for over 27 years. She currently resides in London, Ontario, Canada, with her husband and two cats.

9 781641 526456